Sex-Education

Maurice A. Bigelow

Copyright © BiblioLife, LLC

BiblioLife Reproduction Series: Our goal at BiblioLife is to help readers, educators and researchers by bringing back in print hard-to-find original publications at a reasonable price and, at the same time, preserve the legacy of literary history. The following book represents an authentic reproduction of the text as printed by the original publisher and may contain prior copyright references. While we have attempted to accurately maintain the integrity of the original work(s), from time to time there are problems with the original book scan that may result in minor errors in the reproduction, including imperfections such as missing and blurred pages, poor pictures, markings and other reproduction issues beyond our control. Because this work is culturally important, we have made it available as a part of our commitment to protecting, preserving and promoting the world's literature.

All of our books are in the "public domain" and some are derived from Open Source projects dedicated to digitizing historic literature. We believe that when we undertake the difficult task of re-creating them as attractive, readable and affordable books, we further the mutual goal of sharing these works with a larger audience. A portion of BiblioLife profits go back to Open Source projects in the form of a donation to the groups that do this important work around the world. If you would like to make a donation to these worthy Open Source projects, or would just like to get more information about these important initiatives, please visit www.bibliolife.com/opensource.

SEX-EDUCATION

A SERIES OF LECTURES CONCERNING
KNOWLEDGE OF SEX IN ITS RE-
LATION TO HUMAN LIFE

BY

MAURICE A. BIGELOW

PROFESSOR OF BIOLOGY AND DIRECTOR OF THE SCHOOL
OF PRACTICAL ARTS, TEACHERS COLLEGE
COLUMBIA UNIVERSITY

New York
THE MACMILLAN COMPANY
1916

All rights reserved

LIBRARY
SCRIPPS INSTITUTION
OF OCEANOGRAPHY
UNIVERSITY OF CALIFORNIA
LA JOLLA, CALIFORNIA

COPYRIGHT, 1916,
BY THE MACMILLAN COMPANY.

Set up and electrotyped. Published June, 1916.

Norwood Press
J. S. Cushing Co. — Berwick & Smith Co.
Norwood, Mass., U.S.A.

To
THE MEMORY OF
DR. PRINCE A. MORROW
WHOSE GREAT FAITH IN THE ESSENTIAL GOODNESS OF HUMAN
NATURE LED HIM TO BELIEVE THAT THE PROBLEMS OF
SEX HAVE ARISEN FROM IGNORANCE AND
THAT EDUCATION IS THE KEY TO
THEIR SOLUTION

PREFATORY NOTE

MANY of the lectures printed in this volume have formed the basis of a series given at Teachers College, Columbia University, during the summer sessions of 1914 and 1915, and during the academic year 1914–1915. Others were addressed to parents, to groups of men, to women's clubs, and to conferences on sex-education. In order to avoid extensive repetition, there has been some combination and rearrangement of lectures that originally were addressed to groups of people with widely different outlooks on the sexual problems.

Several years ago the late Dr. Prince A. Morrow announced that a volume dealing with many of the timely topics of sex-education was to be prepared by the undersigned with the advice and criticism of a committee of the American Federation for Sex-Hygiene; but even before Dr. Morrow's death it became evident that this plan was impracticable. Three members (Morrow, Balliet, Bigelow) of the original committee collaborated in a report presented at the XV International Congress on Hygiene and Demography. Since that time the writer, working independently, has found it desirable to reorganize completely the original outline announced by Dr. Morrow.

PREFATORY NOTE

In accordance with a declaration made voluntarily in a conversation with Dr. Morrow, the author considers himself pledged to devote all royalties from this book to the movement for sex-education.

Among the many persons to whom is due acknowledgment of helpfulness in the preparation of this book, the author is especially indebted for suggestions to the late Dr. Prince A. Morrow, to Dr. William F. Snow, Secretary of the American Social Hygiene Association, and to Dr. Edward L. Keyes, Jr., President of the Society of Sanitary and Moral Prophylaxis; for constructive criticism, to his colleagues, Professor Jean Broadhurst and Miss Caroline E. Stackpole, of Teachers College, who have read carefully both the original lectures and the completed manuscript; and to Olive Crosby Whitin (Mrs. Frederick H. Whitin), executive secretary of the Society of Sanitary and Moral Prophylaxis, who has suggested and criticized helpfully both as a reader of the manuscript and as an auditor of many of the lectures delivered at Teachers College.

M. A. B.

TEACHERS COLLEGE,
COLUMBIA UNIVERSITY,
December 28, 1915.

SUMMARY OF CONTENTS

		PAGE
I.	THE MEANING, NEED, AND SCOPE OF SEX-EDUCATION	1

§ 1. Sex-education and its relation to sex-hygiene and social hygiene. § 2. The misunderstanding of sex. § 3. The need of sex-instruction. § 4. The scope of sex-education.

II.	THE PROBLEMS FOR SEX-EDUCATION . .	28

§ 5. Sex problems and the need of special knowledge. § 6. First problem: Personal sex-hygiene. § 7. Second problem: Social diseases. § 8. Third problem: Social evil. § 9. Fourth problem: Illegitimacy. § 10. Fifth problem: Sexual morality. § 11. Sixth problem: Sexual vulgarity. § 12. Seventh problem: Marriage. § 13. Eighth Problem: Eugenics. § 14. Summary.

III.	ORGANIZATION OF EDUCATIONAL ATTACK ON THE SEX PROBLEMS	90

§ 15. The task of sex-education. § 16. The aims of sex-education. § 17. The aims as the basis of organized sex-instruction.

IV.	THE TEACHER OF SEX-KNOWLEDGE . .	108

§ 18. Who should give sex-instruction? § 19. The child's first teachers of sex-

ix

knowledge. § 20. Selecting teachers for class instruction. § 21. Certain undesirable teachers for special hygienic and ethical instruction.

V. BOOKS AS TEACHERS CONCERNING SEX AND LIFE 121
§ 22. Value and danger of special sex-books for young people. § 23. General literature and sex problems. § 24. Dangers in literature on sexual abnormality.

VI. SEX-INSTRUCTION FOR PRE-ADOLESCENT YEARS 133
§ 25. Elementary instruction and influence. § 26. Hygienic and educational treatment of unhealthful habits.

VII. SEX-INSTRUCTION FOR EARLY ADOLESCENT YEARS 146
§ 27. The biological foundations. § 28. Scientific facts for boys. § 29. Scientific facts for girls.

VIII. SPECIAL SEX-INSTRUCTION FOR ADOLESCENT BOYS AND YOUNG MEN 156
§ 30. Developing attitude towards womanhood. § 31. Developing ideals of love and marriage. § 32. Reasons for pre-marital continence. § 33. Essential knowledge concerning prostitution. § 34. Need of refinement of men. § 35. Dancing as a sex problem for men. § 36. Dress of women as a sex problem for men. § 37. The problem of self-control for young men. § 38. The mental side of a young man's sexual life.

CONTENTS

		PAGE
IX.	SPECIAL INSTRUCTION FOR MATURING YOUNG WOMEN	184

§ 39. The young woman's attitude towards manhood. § 40. The young woman's attitude towards love and marriage. § 41. Reasons for pre-marital continence of young women. § 42. Need of optimistic and æsthetic views of sex by women. § 43. Other problems for young women.

X.	CRITICISMS OF SEX-EDUCATION . . .	203

§ 44. A plea for reticence — Agnes Repplier. § 45. A plea for religious approach — Cosmo Hamilton. § 46. The conflict between sex-hygiene and sex-ethics — Richard Cabot. § 47. The arrogance of the advocates of sex-education — William H. Maxwell. § 48. Lubricity in education — W. H. Taft. § 49. Conclusions from the criticisms of sex-education.

XI.	THE PAST AND THE FUTURE OF THE SEX-EDUCATION MOVEMENT	227

§ 50. The American movement. § 51. Important steps. § 52. The future of the larger sex-education.

XII.	SOME BOOKS FOR SEX-EDUCATION . . .	238
INDEX	. . . .	249

I

The Meaning, Need, and Scope of Sex-Education

§ 1. *Sex-education and Its Relation to Sex-hygiene and Social Hygiene*

Sex-education in its largest sense includes all scientific, ethical, social, and religious instruction and influence which directly and in- **Definition** directly may help young people pre- **of sex-** pare to solve for themselves the prob- **education.** lems of sex that inevitably come in some form into the life of every normal human individual. Note the carefully guarded phrase "help young people prepare to solve for themselves the problems of sex", for, like education in general, special sex-education cannot possibly do more than help the individual prepare to face the problems of life.

Now, sex-education as thus defined is more extensive than sex-hygiene, which term was originally applied to instruction concerning sex. **More than** Sex-hygiene obviously refers to health **sex-hygiene.** as influenced by sexual processes, and as such it is a convenient subdivision of the science of health. It would be quite satisfactory as a name for popular instruction concerning sex if that were strictly, or even primarily, hygienic; but in a later lecture it will be shown that the most desirable sex-instruction is only in a minor part a problem of hygiene. I realize that this statement may be declared heretical by many of the present-day advocates of sex-hygiene, because they have approached this latest educational movement from the standpoint of physical health, and especially because their attention has been drawn to the very common occurrence of pathological conditions. Nevertheless, the sexual problems of our times do not all affect physical health, which hygiene aims to conserve; and the sex-educational movement will be quite inadequate without great stress upon certain ethical, social, and other aspects of sex. Young people need instruction that relates not only to health but also to attitude and to morals as these three are influenced by sexual instincts and relationships. This idea will be developed later, but I anticipate here simply to suggest the point of view of the statement that "sex-hygiene" is altogether too limited as a general designation for the desirable instruction concerning sex. The continued use of the term "sex-hygiene," now that the scope of the desirable sex-instruction has been extended far beyond the accepted limits of the science of health, is tending to cause confusion. The educational problems will be more definite and the support of the intelligent public more assured if we limit the use of "sex-hygiene" to the specific problems of health as affected by sexual processes and cease trying to make it include those phases of sex-instruction which have nothing directly to do with health.

Two general terms, "sex-instruction" and "sex-education," are available as all-inclusive designations of the desirable instruction concerning any aspects of sex. They are quite free from the above objections to "sex-hygiene," and it is highly desirable that they should be used in all educational discussions where there is no specific reference to the problems of health. Sex-hygiene will be used in these lectures only when there is some direct reference to health as influenced by the sexual functions.

Social hygiene in its complete sense means the great general movement for the improvement of the conditions of life in all lines in which there is social ill health or need of social reform; but it is often limited to the sexual aspect of the unfortunate and unfavorable conditions of life, and it has been proposed to adopt the term "social hygiene" as a substitute that avoids the word "sex" in sex-hygiene. For this reason it has been incorporated into the names of several societies that are interested in sex-hygiene (*e.g.*, the American Social Hygiene Association). Probably the relation of sex-hygiene to the so-called "social evil" has suggested the use of social hygiene in its most limited sense. It will be unfortunate if this usage becomes so prominent that we think of the health problems of society as chiefly sexual, for the larger outlook of Ellis's "Task of Social Hygiene" is desirable. Likewise, the phrase "social evil" in the sense of sexual evil misleadingly suggests that the only evil of society is the sexual one, but this evasive designation is being supplanted by the more definite and franker word "prostitution."

It should be noted that "social hygiene" as a substitute for "sex-hygiene" is narrower in that it does not include the personal problems of health as affected by sexual processes. This is a serious omission, for certainly all sex-hygiene taught before the later adolescent years should be personal and not social.

Phases of sex-education. The relation of sex-hygiene or social hygiene as a limited phase of sex-education is shown by the following outline:

In the broadest outlook, sex-education (or sex-instruction) includes:		
	sex-hygiene (personal, social)	for sexual health
	biology (including physiology) of reproduction	for attitude regarding sex, and for important scientific facts
	heredity and eugenics	for sexual conduct leading to race improvement
	ethics and sociology of sex	for sexual conduct
	psychology of sex	for sexual health and conduct
	æsthetics of sex	for attitude

Since the original purpose of sex was perpetuation of plant and animal species, and since in the study of biology the idea of sex is illustrated and developed by examination of the reproductive processes in various types, it has been customary for many writers on sex-education to use the terms "sex" and "reproduction" as if they were synonymous. This is no longer so in human life; for while reproduction is a sexual process, sexual activities and influences are often quite unrelated to reproduction. In fact, most of the big problems that have made sex-education desirable, if not necessary, are problems of sex apart from reproduction. It therefore seems clear that, while studies of reproduction are prominent in sex-education, they should be regarded as introductory to the problems of sex, especially for young people. *Sex and reproduction.*

§ 2. *The Misunderstanding of Sex*

Some educators have expressed the wish that some one might suggest a satisfactory substitute for the terms "sex-hygiene" and "sex-education," omitting the word "sex." This word and its companion "sexual" are objectionable because they are associated in the minds of most people with vulgar interpretation of the physical aspects of the beginning of individual life, and much of the opposition to the proposed sex-instruction in home and schools is evidently based on the feeling that the very word "sex" involves something inherently vulgar. *Objection to word "sex."*

It is probable that many decades will pass before the majority of intelligent people cease to feel that

Definite words necessary. the words "sex" and "sexual" have had such vulgar associations that they should be kept out of our everyday vocabulary, but I can see no hope of developing an improved attitude towards the sexual aspect of human life if we continue to admit that we are afraid of the necessary words. It seems to me that in one decade there has been a great advance in that the scientific writers and speakers on problems of sex have been using words which definitely and directly express the desired meanings, and have avoided the suggestive circumlocutions which characterize many modern realistic novels. One who does not already appreciate the serious impressiveness of cold scientific language in discussion of sexual problems should take one of the indecently suggestive paragraphs from stories in the most notoriously vulgar of the fifteen-cent magazines, and translate the meaning of the paragraph into direct and definite words. The result will be complete loss of the stealthy suggestiveness which has made concealed sexuality so dangerously attractive to the type of mind that revels in the modern sex-problem novels. We want no such suggestive concealment in a scheme of sex-education, for it aims at a purer and higher understanding of sex in human life. We must have direct and definite and dignified scientific language, and among the necessary words none are as essential as "sex" and "sexual." We must use them freely if attitude towards sex is to be improved; and their dignified and scientific usage will gradually dispel the embarrassment which many unfortunate people now experience when these words remind them that the perpetuation of life in all its higher forms has been intrusted to the coöperation of two kinds, or sexes, of individuals.

Thus viewing the objections which have been raised against the use of the word "sex" in the educational movement, I have shifted my first stand with the opposition until now I favor the frank and dignified use of this and similar words on appropriate occasions. I believe that those interested in the search for solutions of the vital problems of sex should quietly but systematically work to include the words "sex" and "sexual" in the dignified and scientific vocabulary needed by all people to express the newer and nobler interpretations of the relationships between men and women.

Of course, this does not mean that sex, either as a word or as a fact of nature, should be over-emphasized with people who are too young to appreciate the fundamental facts of life. As already suggested, it is not desirable that any parts of the curricula for schools should be known to the pupils as "sex" studies; but we need such terms as "sex-hygiene" and "sex-instruction" to indicate to teachers and parents that certain parts of the education of the children are being directed towards a healthy, natural and wholesome relation to sex.

No "sex" studies.

It is absurd to suppose that the free, dignified, and scientific use of the word "sex" is going to make people more sensual, more uncontrolled, and more immoral. There is much more reason for fearing the free use of the word "love," which has both psychical and physical meanings so confused that often only the context of sentences enables one to determine which meaning is intended. In fact, many writers and speakers seek to avoid all possible misunderstanding by using the word "affection" for psychical love. Now, in spite of such confusion, and the fact that to many people the word "love" in connection with sex suggests only gross sensuality, we continue to use it freely and it is one of the first words taught to children. Why then do we not hear protests against using the word "love"? Simply because we have been from childhood accustomed to the word, first in its psychical sense, and it is only later that most of us have learned that it has a sensual meaning to some people. In short, familiarity with the word "love" in its psychical sense has bred in us a contempt for those who mistake the physical basis of love for love in its combined physical and psychical completeness.

To many it is surprising to find that the word "sex" has never been used in such degraded connections as has the word "love," and that it has not been half so much misunderstood. There is no obvious vulgarity in the lexicographer's definitions of the word "sex." It simply means, as the science of biology points out so clearly, that the perpetuation of human life, and of most other species of life, has been intrusted to pairs of individuals which are of the two kinds commonly called the sexes, male and female. Why nature determined that each new life in the vast majority of species should develop from two other lives has long been a biological puzzle, and most satisfactory of the answers given is that bi-parental origin of new individuals allows for new combinations of heritable qualities from two lines of descent. However, such a biological explanation of the relation of the two sexes to double parentage is of relatively little practical significance in present-day human life when compared with the fact that out of the necessity for life's perpetuation by two coöperating individuals there has grown psychical or spiritual love with all its splendid possibilities that are evident in ideal family life. Moreover, the influence of sex in human life has extended far beyond the family (that is, that group of individuals who stand related to one another as husband, wife, parents, and children), for it is a careless observer indeed who does not note in our daily life many social and psychical relationships of men and women who have no mutual interests relating to the biological processes of race perpetuation. Of course, the psychologist recognizes that far back of the platonic contact of the sexes on social and intellectual lines is the suppressed and primal instinct that provides physical unions for race perpetuation. However, this is of no practical interest, for, as a matter of fact, the primal instincts are quite subconscious in the usual social relations between the sexes.

There is grandeur in this view of sex as originally a provision for perpetuation of life by two coöperating individuals, later becoming the basis of conjugal affection of the two individuals for each other and of their parental affection for their offspring, and finally leading to social and intellectual comradeship of men and women meeting on terms which are practically free from the original and biological meaning of sex.

The larger view of sex.

Instead, then, of trying to keep sex, both word and fact, in the background of the new educational movement, I believe it is best to work definitely for a better understanding of the part which sex plays in human life, as outlined in the preceding paragraph. Hence, in these lectures I shall never go aside in order to avoid either the word or the idea of sex; on the contrary, I shall attempt to direct the discussion so as to emphasize the larger and very modern view of the relationship of sex and human life.

In this first lecture I want to make it clear that the rôle of sex in human life is vastly greater than that directly involved in sexual activity. I shall in several lectures touch the big problems from the standpoint of the sexual instincts as these play an important part in social, psychical, and æsthetic life even if they are rarely exercised, physiologically, or if, as in millions of individuals, they never come to mean more than possibilities of sexual activity for which opportunities in marriage do not come. I am especially anxious to avoid the nar- row viewpoint of numerous writers on sex-hygiene who seem to overlook the fact that sexual functioning is only a prominent incident in the cycle of sexual influences in the lives of most people. Human life, and especially marriage, should no longer be regarded from the mere biological point of view as for the sole purpose of reproductive activity. It is a far more uplifting view that the conscious or unconscious existence of the sexual instincts, with or without occasional activity, affords the fundamental physical basis for states of mind that may profoundly affect the whole course of life in every normal man and woman. *[The many-sided bearings of sex.]*

Supplementary to this section on the "Misunderstanding of Sex," I suggest the reading of Chapters I–VI of "Sex" by Geddes and Thomson, the "Problems of Sex" by the same authors, and Chapter VI in "The Wonder of Life" by Thomson.

§ 3. *The Need of Sex-Instruction*

The time-honored policy has been one of silence and mystery concerning all things sexual. Everything in that line has long been considered impure and degraded and, therefore, the less said and the less known, the better, especially for young people. Such has been the almost universal attitude of parents until within the present century, when many *[The old silence and the new enlightenment.]*

have awakened to the fact that the policy of silence has been a gigantic failure, because it has not preserved purity and innocence and because it has allowed grave evils, both hygienic and moral, to develop under the cloak of secrecy.

"I don't believe in teaching my boys and girls any facts concerning sex. I prefer to keep them innocent until they have grown up." In these decisive words a prominent woman closed a statement of her firm conviction that the world-wide movement for the sex-instruction of young people is a stupendous mistake. Poor deluded mother! How does she expect to keep her children ignorant of the world of life around them? Is she planning to transplant them to a deserted island where they may grow up innocently? Or is she going to keep the children in some cloister within whose walls there will be immunity from the contamination of the great busy world outside? Or is she going to have them guarded like crown princes, and if so, where are absolutely safe guards to be found? Such are the questions which rush into the minds of those who have studied the problem of keeping children ignorant of the most significant facts of life. It is usually an easy matter to protect children against smallpox and typhoid and some other diseases, but no parent or educator has yet found out how we may be sure to keep real live children ignorant of sex knowledge. They seem to absorb such forbidden facts as naturally and as freely as the air

Children will not remain ignorant.

they breathe. Ask any large group of representative men — ministers, or doctors, or teachers, or men of business, or the world's toilers — whether any of them knew the essential facts of sexual life before they were twelve years of age, and ninety-seven in every hundred will answer quickly in the affirmative. Ask any large group of women, excepting those whose girlhood has been guarded with exceptional care, and the overwhelming majority will acknowledge that they knew the essential facts before they were fifteen years old. Once more, ask these same men and women whether their early knowledge of sex came from pure and reliable sources or from vulgar playmates and depraved servants; and with rare exceptions it is found that vulgarity made the strongest impression in the first lessons concerning the great facts of life. Such being the truth, it is nonsense for parents to sit in complacency because they feel sure that their children are safely protected against any vulgar first lessons concerning sex; for no one can know that children are safely guarded from others who may corrupt their innocent minds. As an illustration, a few years ago the mothers of a group of little girls in one of the best-managed private schools felt that with careful supervision both in school and home there was no danger of forbidden knowledge reaching the children. But one day a new pupil innocently exhibited to her mother a miniature notebook with unprintable notes on sexual topics. The resulting investigation revealed a secret club organized by the pupils for the purpose of passing to each member through notebooks all newly acquired information, which had a peculiar value because it must be kept secret from teachers and parents. That club had been in existence during two school years. This is only a sample case of many which have proved that if children are allowed the freedom that developing individuality demands, their mothers must not feel too sure that their darlings are protected against knowledge of life, and perhaps of life in its most degraded aspects.

Here, then, is the fact that every parent should ponder seriously: Normal children are almost certain to get sexual information not later than the early adolescent years, and usually from unreliable and vulgar sources. It is, therefore, not a question whether children of school ages should be taught the important facts of sex, but whether parents and trained teachers rather than playmates and other unreliable persons should be the instructors. Which will parents choose for their own children? Thousands of intelligent parents have already faced this question, and have decided that their children shall have early sex-instruction in home or school or both in order that there will be little danger of vulgar impressions taking a deep hold on child minds.

The vital question for parents.

Granted, then, that children should be given some reliable instruction concerning things sexual, who should be the teacher, what should be taught, and when should the instruction be given? These are the fundamental questions now being considered by the parents and educators who have accepted sex-education as necessary. Upon the final answers to such questions the decision of many parents will depend. I shall attempt to answer them in later lectures.

The policy of maintaining mystery and secrecy concerning sex has failed with adults even more sadly than with children. Health and morals have suffered incalculable injury. The sexual evils of our time are not as bad as were those of the ancient civilizations, but we have little reason to be proud of the slight progress made. But why should we expect the human race to make progress when sexual problems have been kept in darkness? *Sex mystery has prevented progress.* The wonder is that, with the prevailing dark outlook on sexual life throughout the past nineteen centuries, the world has not developed more sexual vice. Innate animalistic appetites have tended to lead downward, and surely the policy of silence has offered no counteracting influence towards higher living. While religion and ethics, by means of certain rules of conduct, have maintained certain sexual standards, they have not kept vast numbers of humans from falling far below those standards into utter degradation. The modern teachers of religion and ethics have prevented general sexual degradation, but they have failed to give human sexuality any decided uplift. The reason for this failure is the policy of mystery and silence. The teachers of religion and ethics have preferred to let general and more or less abstruse rules govern conduct in sexual lines. Until recent years there have been few sermons in which common sexual problems have been presented so that the preacher's meaning has been clear to all. On the contrary, there has been universal mystery and evasion concerning the greatest facts of life.

Many people have justified the mystery thrown around sexual processes on the theory that the reproductive instincts of mature people are sufficient guides for conduct. This involves a misunderstanding of sexual instincts of the higher mammals which are often unscientifically cited as models for human imitation. In these animals sexual union is instinctively determined, because normally the sexual hunger or excitement of both sexes is stimulated and controlled by the physiological condition of the female at the times favorable for fertilization (*i.e.*, at the œstrual periods). For example, a pair of dogs living in close companionship show signs of mutual sexual desires only for a few days at the semi-annual œstrual or fertile periods of the female. It occasionally happens that the males of various wild and domesticated mammals exhibit signs of automatic sexual excitement (*i.e.*, not caused by the stimulus arising from the physiological condition of the female); but in such cases of male excitement outside of the mating or œstrual periods, the normal females invariably offer instinctive opposition to attempted union by abnormally or automatically

Sexual instincts offer no guidance.

excited males. Thus, directly and indirectly, there is instinctive control and limitation of sexual union among the animals that are most closely related to the human race.

It is biologically possible that similar conditions may have existed in the earliest human life, but that is pure speculation and has no bearing on the practical problems of sex in human life to-day. The fact is that the simple physiological stimuli which produce sexual excitement in both sexes of animals have practically no influence in determining human sexual union. On the contrary, memory associations consciously connected with the opposite sex, especially those associations that are centered in affection, may at any time in the normal individual of either human sex afford the basis for a chain of mental states leading to sexual excitement and union. There is not, as in the animals, instinctive dependence on the physiological conditions that are favorable for fertilization. In fact, spontaneous physiological demands play in civilized human life a minor part in initiating sexual excitement. The reason why some humans seem to have unusual sexual intensity is not so much a matter of exceptionally strong sexuality as of susceptibility to the numerous sexual stimuli with which modern life abounds. For this reason, a man who has formed lewd memory associations is more susceptible to sexual stimulations, *e.g.*, by obscene pictures, vulgar words, unusual dress or actions of women, close physical association as in dancing, and certain forms of music. It is not at all uncommon that individuals who are hypersensitive to sexually suggestive stimuli are really functionally weak.

It follows from the facts outlined above that instinctive control of sexual actions applies to animals but not to human life. On the contrary, human control must be on the basis of intelligent choice. This means the greatest task of human life, for it **Intelligent control only.** requires voluntary control of instinctive demands which are intensified by numerous stimuli or temptations that are exclusively human. No wonder that natural sex hunger left uncontrolled leads human beings to excesses and degradation that no species of animals with their guiding instincts could possibly reach.

The absence from human life of any instinctive control of sexual actions leaves a great responsibility **Individual responsibility.** on each individual whose natural desires lead impulsively and insistently towards sexual union and must be restrained, controlled, and directed by voluntary choice. In short, all individuals who are intelligent beings are personally responsible for voluntary control of their sexual desires with reference to the ethical, social, and eugenic interests and rights of all other individuals now and in the future.

With such an understanding of instincts in relation to human sexual actions, we cannot wonder that the old policy of mystery has failed so completely. Since human beings are left to control the most powerful appetite by intelligence, it is evident that a policy based on silence, ignorance, and mystery must fail. The only safe and sure road to the needed control of sexual actions is to be found in knowledge, and the widespread recognition of this fact has led to the new movement for general enlightenment regarding sexual processes in their various relations to human life. *Sexual knowledge necessary.*

It is not surprising that we have turned to seek an educational solution for the problems of sex. Education has become the modern panacea for many of our ills — hygienic, industrial, political, and social. We have found people losing health for various reasons and we have proposed hygienic instruction as a prophylactic. We have analyzed many problems of the industries, and now we are beginning to seek their solution in industrial education. We have noted that numerous social and political misunderstandings check progress of individuals and nations, and we are coming to think the pathway upwards is to be found in better knowledge of social and political science. And, in like manner, in every phase of this modern life of ours we are looking to knowledge as the key to all significant problems. It is truly the age of education, not simply the education offered in schools and colleges, but education in the larger sense, including the learning of useful knowledge from all sources whatsoever. *Education as a solution of sex problems.*

With such unbounded confidence in the all-sufficiency of education, it is most natural that we should turn to it in these times when we have come to realize the existence of amazing sexual problems caused either by ignorant misuse, or by deliberate abuse, of the sexual functions which biologically are intrusted with the perpetuation of human life and which psychologically are the source of human affection in its supreme forms. If education is to solve the civic, hygienic, and industrial problems of to-day and to-morrow, why should it not also help with the age-old sexual evils? So reasoning, we have naturally turned to education as one, but not the only, method of attack on the sexual problems which have degraded and devitalized human life of all past times, but which somehow have kept out of the limelight of publicity until our own times.

§ 4. *The Scope of Sex-education*

It is well to make clear in this first lecture that no one proposes to limit sex-instruction to schools and colleges. We may safely leave mathematics and writing and even reading to schools, but sex-education will fail unless the schools can get the coöperation of the homes, the churches, the Y.M.C.A., the Y.W.C.A., the W.C.T.U., the Boy Scouts, the Camp Fire Girls, and other organizations which aim to reach young people socially, religiously, and ethically. The part which these have already taken in the sex-education movement is in the aggregate far more important than what the schools

Sex-education is not primarily for schools.

have been able to accomplish. Sex-education, then, should be understood as including all serious instruction — no matter where or when or by whom given — which aims to help young people face the problems that normal sexual processes bring to every life.

In a later lecture I shall urge the importance of beginning sex-instruction in the home. There are some parents who wish that it were possible not only to begin but also to end it there, for they fear that public instruction will lead to a weakening of a certain sense of reserve and privacy that has long been considered sacred to the best family life. Perhaps this has some truth, but we must remember that only in rare homes are there such ideal relationships of parents to each other and to their offspring that matters of sex are sacred to the family circle. The fact which parents and educators must face is that there are now relatively few homes in which there is one parent able to begin the elementary instruction of young children; and, therefore, as a practical matter for the best interests of the vast majority of young people, we must consider ways and means for instruction outside of most homes. This need not interfere in the least with the parents who are able and willing to give sex-instruction to the children, for the home instruction will naturally anticipate that which the schools must give for the pupils who are not properly instructed at home. It seems to me to be a situa-

Sex-instruction impossible in most homes.

tion like that of children learning to read at home and later continuing reading at school. Sex-instruction begun at home will form the child's attitude and give him some elementary information, and later he may profitably learn more in the same lines in the class work of school, especially in connection with science instruction for which few homes have facilities. Moreover, it is quite possible that one instructed at home in childhood may gain from later school instruction something of great social value, for we must remember that the problems of sex which most demand attention are not individual, but social. Hence, it may be worth while for the home-instructed individual to learn through class instruction that people outside the home look seriously upon knowledge concerning sexual processes, and that every individual's life must be adjusted to other lives, that is, to society.

Summarizing, it appears that however desirable home instruction regarding sex may be, the majority of parents are not able and willing to undertake the work, and so the public educational system and organizations for social and religious work should provide a scheme of instruction which will make sure that all young people will have an opportunity to get the most helpful information for the guidance of their lives.

In order to gain the serious attention of those who believe themselves unalterably opposed to school instruction regarding things sexual, I anticipate a later discussion and mention in this connection that there must be great caution in all attempts at school teaching that directly touches human sexual life. It would be a dangerous experiment to introduce sex-instruction into all schools by sudden legislation. There must be specially trained teachers of selected personality and tact. No existing high school has enough such teachers, and in the grammar schools where the pupils are at the age when proper instruction would influence them most, the problem of general class instruction is absolutely unsolved. Only here and there in schools below the high school has a teacher or principal of rare quality made satisfactory experimental teaching. So uncertain are we at present regarding how we should approach the problem of teaching grammar-school children that the only safe advice for general use is that teachers, or preferably principals, should begin with parents' conferences led by one who is a conservative expert on sex-instruction. Were I principal of a school with pupils from, say, two hundred and fifty homes, I should begin at once to organize conferences designed to awaken the parents to the need of sex-instruction for their children, and to the importance of making at least a beginning in the homes. I should expect, according to the experience of others, that of the five hundred parents, two hundred mothers and fifty fathers would take an interest in the conferences, and that at least one hundred fathers too busy for meetings would approve heartily

Caution in school instruction.

Parents' co-operation.

after hearing reports from their wives. Thus, I should try to reach the majority of homes represented in my school. I should be in no hurry to introduce class instruction — I mean instruction related directly to human life; but, of course, I should encourage my teachers to emphasize the life-histories of animals and plants in the nature-study, and so lay in the pupils' minds a firm foundation for later connection between human life and all life. At the same time, I should keep my teachers on the lookout for individual pupils or groups that might need special attention and, if such be found, I should seek the coöperation of their parents. And finally, after a year or two of co-working with parents, I should hope to get permission for special talks based on nature-study and hygiene. These talks should first be given to limited groups of pupils, preferably in the presence of some parents who are interested and who have given their children some home instruction. Working along such conservative lines, I believe a tactful principal of a grammar school might succeed in developing much of the needed instruction for pre-adolescent pupils.

With regard to high-school pupils, we should remember that nine-tenths of the desirable information is already included in the biology of our best high schools. The remaining tenth is that which connects all life with human life; and this requires tact and exceptional skill. However, the high schools no longer

Instruction in high schools.

offer an insoluble problem, for many teachers have succeeded in giving the desirable instruction to the satisfaction of critical principals and parents.

There is a widespread impression that sex-instruction should begin with the approach of adolescence and soon be completed. This idea is often expressed by parents and even by prominent educators who say that the father or teacher ought "to take the boy of thirteen aside and tell him some things he ought to know." Still others have the same point of view when they advocate that a physician should be called for a lecture to high-school boys. In fact, most people who have not seriously studied the problems of sex-education seem to believe that one concentrated dose of sex-instruction in adolescent years is sufficient guidance for young people. *Sex-education from early childhood to maturity.*

Such limited personal instruction might suffice if sex-education were limited to sex-hygiene. A few hygienic commands in pre-adolescent years and one impressive talk in early puberty might teach the boy or girl how not to interfere with health; but it is improbable that such brief instruction will make a permanent impression which will insure hygienic practice of the precepts laid down. If we hold that sex-hygiene is important, then it must be drilled into the learner from several points of view. An isolated lesson on any topic of general hygiene is of very doubtful efficiency.

The most important reason why sex-instruction should not be concentrated in a short period of youth is that it is impossible to exert the most desirable influence upon health, attitude, and morals except by instruction beginning in early childhood and graded for each period of life up to maturity. Most young people who in early adolescence receive their first lessons from parents and teachers have already had their attitude formed by their playmates. Even their morals may become corrupted and their health irreparably injured several years before puberty. The only sure pathway to health, attitude, and morals is in beginning with young children and instructing them as gradually as the problems of sex come forward.

Brief instruction does not fix attitude.

The greatest possible good of sex-education will not be secured if it stops with early adolescent years. There are many problems of sex in relation to society, particularly in relation to monogamic marriage, that young people should be led to consider in the late teens and early twenties. Our sex-education system will not be completely organized until we find ways and means for carrying the instruction by lectures, conferences, and books beyond the years commonly occupied by public-school education. Colleges and other higher educational institutions may contribute somewhat to this advanced sex-instruction; but obviously the great majority of maturing young people cannot be reached personally except by instruction arranged in churches, the Y.M.C.A., and the Y.W.C.A., evening schools, and other

Sex-instruction after youth.

such institutions. In many respects this proposed instruction for maturing young people is of very great importance and deserves encouragement such as has not yet been given by those who have written and lectured in favor of a movement for sex-education of young people.

In conclusion of this introductory lecture, let me say that I have tried to suggest in a general survey that sex-education in its largest outlook touches great problems of life in very many ways. I have also tried to convince that it is far more than merely a school subject, limited entirely to a curriculum extended over a few years. This is the common misunderstanding arising from the familiar use of the word "education." As opposed to this narrow conception, I understand sex-education, the larger sex-education, to be a collective term designating all organized effort, both in and out of schools, toward instructing and influencing young people with regard to the problems of sex. Here we have returned to the central thought of the definition with which this lecture opened, and which I emphasize because it is the foundation of all future lectures: The larger sex-education includes all scientific, ethical, social, and religious instruction and influence which in any way may help young people prepare to meet the problems of life in relation to sex.

The larger sex-education.

II

THE PROBLEMS FOR SEX-EDUCATION

§ 5. *Sex Problems and the Need of Special Knowledge*

In these lectures I shall discuss the great sex problems towards the solution of which knowledge conveyed by special education may help. These problems offer reasons or arguments in favor of sex-education, and I shall attempt to present them from this point of view. I shall at the same time point out in preliminary outline how organized instruction may apply more or less directly to the sex problems that seem to show the need of educational attack, but in later lectures the organization of instruction will be considered more specifically.

Arguments for sex-education.

In reviewing the literature that during the past decade has advocated sex-education, it has seemed to me that there is left little possibility of any decidedly new and important contribution to the arguments favoring such instruction, for the whole case has been splendidly presented by eminent writers in the fields of medicine, biology, sociology, and ethics. It now appears that the great majority of educators, scientists, and intelligent citizens in general have accepted the

Propagandism needed.

arguments for sex-instruction, so far as they have been informed concerning the meaning and need of the movement; and this leads me to the belief that in the future we need not new arguments but frequent restatements of the established facts which indicate the importance of widespread knowledge regarding the function that is inseparably connected with the perpetuation of life. In short, we now need a propagandism for extending the sex-education movement among the masses of people.

For those who have already accepted sex-education, a survey of the facts that created a demand for sex-instruction will give a clearer outlook on the movement. The rapid increase of interest in sex-education has been the result of widespread dissemination of convincing facts concerning some common disharmonies that grow out of the sexual problems of the human race. These facts which have led to sex-education should be kept in mind by all who wish to understand or to play a part in the instruction of young people.

It is quite unnecessary, and still more undesirable, to recite at length in these lectures the social, medical, and psycho-pathological facts concerning abnormal or perverted sexual processes. Fortunately, the educational ends may be gained by a general review that points out the bearings of the main lines of the sexual problems, the misunderstandings and mistakes that education may help prevent and correct.

It is important that the general public, especially the parents, should understand the reasons which have induced numerous physicians, ministers, and educators to become active advocates of systematic sex-instruction for young people. Although the movement has made extensive progress in the ten years of propagandic work, it is probably true that the majority of even intelligent parents are not yet convinced that their children need sex-instruction. This is due largely to the fact that the parents have not yet been shown the reasons why it is now, and always has been, unsafe to allow children to gain more or less sexual information from unreliable and vulgar sources. In fact, it is surprising to find many parents, especially mothers, who seem unable to grasp the idea that their "protected" children can possibly get impure information.

Parents should know reasons for sex-instruction.

There are other parents who know that their children are almost sure to get vulgar information regarding sexual matters, and that some young people are likely to make sexual mistakes; but they calmly look upon such things as part of the established order of the world.

Still another type of parents who should know the reasons for sex-instruction are those who accept the traditional idea that their daughters must be kept "protected" and "innocent" while their sons are free to sow a large field of "wild oats," concerning which society in general, and such parents in particular, will care little as long as social diseases, bastardy suits, or chronic alcoholism do not result from the dissipations. These are the fathers and mothers who need the most enlightenment concerning the importance of such sex-instruction as will make clear the far-reaching consequences of "wild oat sowing." Perhaps most such parents are ignorant, but some are simply thoughtless. As an illustration of the latter, the editor of a well-known magazine was recently talking with a prominent author and made some reference to the immoral habits of young men. Their conversation was essentially as follows: The author remarked, "I assume that my boys will be boys and will have their fling before they settle down and marry." The editor quickly replied, "Yes, and I presume that you expect your boys to sow their wild oats with my daughters, and that in return you will expect my sons to dissipate with your daughters. At any rate, you have damnable designs on somebody's daughters." This put on the wild-oat proposition a light which was apparently new to the literary man, for he replied, "That is a phase of the young man's problem which never occurred to me. It does sound startling when stated in that personal way."

All these classes of parents who have not yet learned the facts which point to ignorance as the cause of the abundant sexual errors of young people and those who do not understand that sexual promiscuity or immorality is an error of gravest significance both to the individual and to society, should have set before them time and again some of the startling facts which in the first five years of the American sex-education movement were promulgated among physicians, ministers, and educators. All such ignorant or indifferent parents will not take an interest in the proposed sex-instruction unless they are convinced by frank and forcible statements regarding the great need of special safeguarding of young people.

Since there are so many people who still need the most elementary knowledge concerning the sexual problems that demand educational attack, it is important that there should be local associations which can manage lectures, publications, conferences, and other means of informing the public as to the gravity of the sexual problems of our times, and as to the part which sex-instruction may play in the attempt at finding a solution. Such work is now being done splendidly by the societies named in § 51. The magnitude of the problem of reaching the public is such that there is abundant work for numerous branches of such societies or for local groups willing to take a part in the needed work. As suggested elsewhere, the success of the movement for sex-instruction of children of school ages will depend largely upon the attitude and coöperation of parents; and hence it is important that parents should be led to understand the reasons or arguments for sex-instruction. In other words, they should know the problems that indicate the importance of enlightening the rising generation concerning the great facts of sex and life.

Special associations needed.

Among the numerous publications that seem to me adapted for convincing parents that their children need instruction, I commonly mention the following: Lowry's "False Modesty" and "Teaching Sex Hygiene," Howard's "Start your Child Right," Wile's "Sex Education," Galloway's "Biology of Sex," March's "Towards Racial Health," Lyttleton's "Training of the Young in Laws of Sex," and pamphlets by Dr. Prince Morrow. See also pages 241–243.

Books for parents.

There are eight important sex problems of our times that offer reasons or arguments for sex-instruction, because ignorance plays a large part in each problem. I shall state them briefly here and discuss each in succeeding lectures: (1) Many people, especially in youth, need hygienic knowledge concerning sexual processes as they affect personal health. (2) There is an alarming amount of the dangerous social diseases which are distributed chiefly by the sexual promiscuity or immorality of many men. (3) The uncontrolled sexual passions of men have led to enormous development of organized and commercialized prostitution. (4) There are living to-day tens of thousands of unmarried mothers and illegitimate children, the result of the common sexual irresponsibility of men and the ignorance of women. (5) There is need of more general following of a definite moral standard regarding sexual relationships. (6) There is a prevailing unwholesome attitude of mind concerning all sexual processes. (7) There is very general misunderstanding of sexual life as related to healthy

Knowledge needed concerning eight sex problems.

D

and happy marriage. (8) There is need of eugenic responsibility for sexual actions that concern future generations.

Here are the eight sexual problems of our times. Any one of them has significance great enough to demand the attention of educators and social reformers. One and all they point to the need of better understanding regarding the sexual functions and their relation to life. I shall now turn to outline the main facts concerning each of these sexual problems so far as it seems likely that they will concern educators and social workers. For convenience I shall use the following brief headings: (1) Personal sex-hygiene, (2) social diseases, (3) social evil, (4) illegitimacy, (5) sexual morality, (6) sexual vulgarity, (7) sexual problems and marriage, (8) eugenics.

These sexual problems toward whose solution special instruction of young people may help are **Historical order.** stated here in the order in which they have attracted attention as reasons for sex-education. Thus, for instance, personal sex-hygiene was the chief reason recognized twenty years ago; social diseases began to attract public attention ten years ago; commercial prostitution has been especially prominent in the discussions of the past five years; and only recently has there been emphasis on sex-education with reference to eugenics.

The historical order which I follow in this lecture is not now the order of greatest importance. For example, sexual morality (5) and vulgarity (6) are probably of far greater significance than any of the other sexual problems that offer arguments for sex-education.

To avoid possible misunderstanding, let me repeat from the first lecture the proposition that sex-education should extend in home and school from childhood to maturity. It follows that these lectures concerning the problems of sex that seriously affect the human race are not all applicable as arguments for instruction in schools or for children of school age. Some of the problems of sex point to the need of special instruction in pre-adolescent or in adolescent years, but some of them concern directly only those who are approaching maturity.

Not all sex problems concern youth.

§ 6. *First Problem for Sex-instruction: Personal Sex-hygiene*

It is convenient to group under personal sex-hygiene all hygienic knowledge concerning sexual processes in their personal as distinguished from their social aspects. The distinction between these two aspects of sex-hygiene is essentially on the same basis as that between personal and public hygiene. For example, indigestion and overwork are matters of personal hygiene, while tuberculosis and typhoid are problems of public hygiene because the individual case leads through infection to disease of others. Similarly, such individual disorders as masturbation and

Personal and social hygiene.

deranged menstruation concern personal health directly, while venereal diseases are clearly included in social sex-hygiene.

If there were no other reasons for sex-instruction, I believe that it would be worth while to teach such hygienic knowledge of self and sex as would guard young people against harmful habits and unhealthful care of their sexual mechanisms; and which, moreover, would guide them across the threshold of adolescence with some helpful understanding of the significance of the metamorphosis. Many men and women suffer from injured, if not ruined, health because they did not know, especially between ten and fourteen years, the laws of personal sex-hygiene, which concern health in ways not involving sexual relationship. Many boys and some girls are injured both physically and mentally by the habit of masturbation. Numerous girls are injured physically and many mentally because they have not learned in advance the nature and hygiene of menstruation. Many boys are injured both in mind and character because they have no scientific guidance which helps them understand themselves during the stormy transition from youth into manhood. Moreover, there are certain simple hygienic commands that children under twelve should receive from parents and teachers. In all these lines the bearings of personal hygienic instruction are so obvious that we need not at this time stop to consider in more detail this first reason or problem for sex-instruction of young people.

Personal sex-hygiene needed.

§ 7. Second Problem for Sex-instruction: Social Diseases

During the past decade the general public has received some astounding revelations concerning the enormous extent of illicit sexual promiscuity, which is immorality according to our commonly accepted code of morals. Along with the evidence as to the existence of widespread promiscuity, has come the still more alarming information from the medical profession that sexual promiscuity commonly distributes the germs of the two highly infectious and exceedingly destructive diseases, syphilis and gonorrhea, known in medical science as venereal or social. When these are acquired by individuals guilty of sexual promiscuity, they seriously and often fatally affect the victim; but of far greater social-hygienic importance is the medical evidence that they are very often transmitted to persons innocent of any transgression of the moral law, especially to wives and children.

Recent publicity regarding vice and disease.

The medical revelations concerning the relation of sexual immorality to the plague of social diseases, has come from certain eminent physicians, notably the late Dr. Prince A. Morrow. His translation of Fournier's "Syphilis and Marriage" (1881), his own "Social Diseases and Marriage" (1904), and several of his pamphlets published by the American Society of Sanitary and Moral Prophylaxis, have been authoritative statements of conditions as the medical world sees them.

The extent of social diseases is a fairly accurate measure of the minimum amount of immorality, for nothing is better established in medical science than that promiscuity in sexual relations is directly or indirectly responsible for spread of the microorganisms which cause the diseases. If for several generations all men and women limited their sexual relations to monogamic marriage, and the relatively rare cases of non-sexual and prenatal infection were treated so as to render them non-contagious, the social diseases would probably disappear from the human family. Such a statement is significant only in showing the relation of social diseases to sexual promiscuity, for of course, there is no reasonable hope that the venereal germs will ever be annihilated by universal monogamy.

Social diseases and immorality.

Reduction of the amount of venereal disease must depend upon (1) hygienic and moral education which will lead people to avoid the sources of infection and (2) sanitary and medical science which works either by applying antiseptic or other prophylactic methods for preventing development of the causative microörganisms, or by using germicides for destroying those germs which have already produced disease. Thus the educational and the sanitary attack on the social diseases lie parallel. Both are needed, for, even with all the possible methods of attack, the progress against these diseases will be exceedingly slow.

Attack by education and sanitation.

Those who are interested in the facts relating to social diseases which point to the need of sex-education as one method of prevention, are referred to the pamphlets published by the American Society of Sanitary and Moral Prophylaxis; Morrow's "Social Diseases and Marriage"; Creighton's "The Social Disease and How to Fight It"; Dock's "Hygiene and Morality"; Henderson's "Education with Reference to Sex"; and certain chapters in Warbasse's "Medical Sociology."

With regard to the accuracy of the commonly quoted statements concerning the prevalence of social disease, and therefore of immorality, it must be said in all fairness that there has been much guesswork and some deliberate exaggeration. *Estimated amount of disease.* We learn from various books and lectures that fifty, sixty-five, seventy-five and even ninety per cent of the men in the United States over eighteen years of age are at some time infected with at least one of the social diseases. The fact is that there is no scientific way of getting accurate statistics, for unlike other contagious diseases, the venereal ones are kept more or less secret, and numerous cases cannot be discovered by health officers. All the published figures regarding the prevalence of such diseases are merely estimates based upon the experience of certain physicians with special groups of men, especially in hospitals. There is no reliable scientific evidence as to the prevalence of venereal disease in the whole mass of our American population.

However, so far as education is concerned, there is nothing to be gained by dispute as to the possible inaccuracy of the higher percentages,[1] for it is generally admitted that probably over fifty per cent of the men in America and Europe become infected with gonorrhea or syphilis, or both, one or more times during their lives, especially in early manhood. This conservative estimate is sufficient to show that the sexual morals of probably the majority of men are at some time in their lives loose. There is reason to believe that with most such men the period of moral laxity is in early manhood before marriage, which, though not excusable, is explainable on physiological grounds. It is important to correct the wrong impression which is now widespread, especially among women who have read the more or less sensational statements in certain books and magazines, that the quoted figures on social disease mean that from fifty to ninety per cent of all men are immoral from time to time for many years. If that were true, the situation represented by the highest estimates would be hopeless, and we might as well start out to adjust society to a system of recognized sexual promiscuity. Fortunately, it is far from true, for a great many men included in

Education not concerned with percentages.

[1] In the *American Journal of Public Health* for July, 1913, Dr. John S. Fulton, Director General of the XV International Congress on Hygiene and Demography, criticized severely the extremely radical statistics that were presented on charts at the sex-hygiene exhibit of the Congress, and were later published in Wilson's "Education of the Young in Sex-hygiene."

even the conservative statistics of social disease were infected because they strayed from the moral path very few times and in many cases only once. This fact makes the outlook for improved sexual morals and health more hopeful, for probably the majority of young men need help in controlling themselves for a few years only, especially between eighteen and twenty-five.[1]

The reports of medical men regarding the damage done by the social diseases are inaccurate chiefly when they attempt to state percentages of the whole population. They are reliable when they state observed facts, such as the following: It is now established in medical science that (1) gonorrheal infection results in tens of thousands of cases in complications, such as heart disease, gonorrheal rheumatism, sterility of both men and women, blindness of infants, inflammatory diseases of female reproductive organs, and other well-marked sequelæ of the disease; and (2) that syphilis is responsible for a large majority of cases of locomotor ataxia, paresis and certain types of insanity, and also for numerous aneurisms of arteries, many apoplexies, and much disease of liver, kidneys, and other organs. Moreover, syphilis is charged with being the greatest race destroyer. Fournier, the great French specialist,

Established facts.

[1] There is danger in quoting to young men the estimates as to prevalence of social diseases and, therefore, of promiscuity. Fear of consequences will not control one who is led to believe that he is doing what most men do. (See Parkinson in *Educational Review*, Jan. 1911, pp. 44-46.)

noted that only two children survived from a series of ninety pregnancies of syphilitic women of the well-to-do class. It is probably true that much less than ten per cent of syphilitized embryos ever grow into mature men and women, and even these few survivors are likely to carry in their bodies the germs or the "virus" of syphilis which may affect the next generation.

Such direct statements as the above may be accepted as not exaggerated. However, it little matters in sex-education, except for the purposes of sensational writers, whether statistics regarding the damage done by venereal diseases are more than estimates; for it is sufficient to remember that every physician of large experience agrees that syphilis and gonorrhea are so common and so destructive of health and life that they must be classed among the most dangerous diseases that now threaten the human race. This ought to be sufficient to attract the serious attention of every thinking man and woman.

Social diseases admittedly dangerous.

Thus, in general survey, we see the great problems of social-sexual hygiene caused by diseases that are widely distributed because sexual instincts are uncontrolled. In short, the alarming problem of the social diseases results from masculine promiscuity or the failure of men to adhere to the monogamic standards of morality. In other and familiar phrasing, there is widespread acceptance and practice of the so-called

Double standard of morality.

"double standard of sexual morality," a monogamic one for respectable women and promiscuity for many of their male relatives and friends. (See writings of Morrow, especially "The Sex Problem"; also Creighton's "The Social Disease.")

Our brief survey of the hygienic problems caused by sexual promiscuity and its characteristic diseases is sufficient to indicate one great problem for sex-education. Such social-hygiene problems have been most responsible for the recent and rapid rise of the movement for sex-education, and they must be recognized in any adequate scheme for instruction of young people.

One problem for sex-education.

Can scientific education hope to solve the sexual problems of society by inculcating such fear of venereal diseases that men will remain true to the monogamic code of morality? Many cynical disbelievers in sex-hygiene answer this question negatively by asking in biblical phrase, "Can the leopard change his spots?" In other words, these doubting ones believe that sexual instincts are so firmly fixed in the nature of *many* men and *some* women that there is no hope of radical change through education.[1] There is something in this point of view. It is probably true that even the most radical advocates of sex-

Is sex-hygiene adequate?

---

[1] Many writers have discounted the value of warnings involved in sex-instruction concerning social disease (see especially Cabot's papers referred to in § 46, and Parkinson in *Educational Review*, January, 1911).

education do not hope to secure universal monogamy and consequent disappearance of social diseases. A conservative and rational answer to the above question whether sex-education can solve the problem of social diseases, is that a large percentage of even civilized people are not yet ready to have their most powerful instincts controlled by scientific knowledge. Hence, there is no hope that the hygienic task of sex-education will be finished soon after instruction becomes an established part of general education in homes and schools. At the very best there will be incomplete returns for the social-hygienic aspect of sex-instruction, but already we know for a certainty that enough young men will be influenced to make the teaching justifiable. I feel sure of this because I have met personally many such men and my friends know many more.

According to the investigations made by Dr. Exner, the medical secretary of the Young Men's Christian Association, a great reduction of venereal disease has followed sex-hygienic campaigns in college towns.

In another way hygienic teaching may reduce the amount of venereal diseases, and that is by leading **Medical treatment.** infected individuals to seek thorough medical treatment without delay. This, of course, will render the diseased person non-infectious to others. Physicians report that there is now a marked movement in this direction and, moreover, that many infected young men voluntarily seek medical examinations before marriage.

Even if we refuse to believe that social-hygienic teaching will protect many young men from sexual diseases, there is the woman's need of information to be considered. As said before, women more than men suffer the consequences of venereal infections. Therefore, every young woman who considers marriage should know the possibility of danger to herself and her children, and be able to decide accordingly. Of course, even with much knowledge she may marry the wrong man, for correct diagnosis of social disease is not always easy; but if her confidence is betrayed and she becomes infected, she ought to know the importance of immediate and radical medical treatment. Let me illustrate these statements that women should know the danger of venereal disease. One of my college friends neglected an important legal case to travel seven hundred miles in order to tell face to face another college friend that she was about to marry a dangerous man. Being utterly ignorant of the existence of sexual diseases, the girl and her mother characterized my friend's statement by a short and ugly word, and ordered him to leave their home instantly. The marriage occurred and some months later the young woman went to her grave, a victim of gonorrheal salpingitis and peritonitis.

Woman's need of information.

Another case which illustrates the danger of a woman's ignorance: One of my students of many years ago married a minister who infected her with syphilis and kept her from medical attention until the disease was in a highly developed stage, and even then conspired with an inefficient doctor to keep her ignorant of the nature of the disease.

These are not extreme cases, for any physician with large experience knows that such things are common. Medical literature is full of such painful recitals of venereal tragedies. It is not desirable that all young women should know the details of such tragedies, but they should know that dangers exist. Parents and educators will not have done their duty until they coöperate to give all young women the protective knowledge they have a right to demand.[1]

The right to knowledge.

There is another way of looking at the possible effect of the social side of sex-hygienic instruction. It is sure to make a decided impression upon many young people of the type that we regard as the best in every way. These will be the leaders of the future and they in turn will help improve conditions. Perhaps it may all work out as the drug problem is being solved. Widespread social and hygienic information regarding the harmful effect of alcohol, cocaine, opium, and other drugs has first of all impressed leading citizens; and these are beginning to control by laws those who cannot be reached directly by education. In some such ways those who are impressed by

Best people must lead.

[1] Louise Creighton, in her excellent little book on "The Social Disease and How to Fight It" (Longmans), has well presented the problems of social impurity from woman's point of view.

Dr. W. S. Hall, in "Life's Problems," has given in a few pages the necessary protective knowledge.

formal sex-education may lend a hand in influencing many who could not be touched directly by hygienic education.

There is no doubt that public enlightenment regarding the dangers of social diseases will soon lead to legislation and public medical work **Legislation** which will contribute greatly towards **needed.** reduction of the diseases. For example, legislation with reference to venereal disease should require doctors to report cases to health officers, should forbid "quack" advertising of fake "cures," should forbid sale by drug stores of nostrums for personal treatment, should provide dispensaries and hospitals for reliable treatment at reasonable cost, should require medical examinations for marriage licenses and provide for such examinations at moderate charges or at public expense, should require certain sanitary precautions in care of eyes of new-born infants, and should provide for discovery and treatment of congenital syphilis in school children. These are lines in which good laws might help vastly in the war against the social diseases. Moreover, it is obvious that all laws which help control the social evil will work indirectly against the social diseases.

In conclusion, it seems probable that popular knowledge of the social side of sex-hygiene will reduce the amount of venereal disease **Probable** (1) by teaching some people the dangers **results of** of promiscuity, (2) by adoption of certain **instruction.** sanitary precautions that lessen danger of infection, (3) by leading people to seek competent medical aid which, while often failing to restore the victim's health, will probably eliminate the danger of contagion for others, and (4) by intelligent support of laws that directly or indirectly affect the social diseases.

I have given great prominence to the social-sexual diseases in their relation to sex-education because along this line there has been developed the widespread interest in sex-instruction as *one* method of protecting young people against promiscuity. So far as the questions of teaching are concerned, my personal view is that some of the other reasons or problems for sex-instruction are more important, because I believe that educational emphasis on them will give the greatest results in improved sexual conditions of society.

Social diseases not most important.

§ 8. *Third Problem for Sex-instruction: the Social Evil*

So far as the problems of sex-education are concerned, there is nothing to be gained by an extensive review of commercialized prostitution. It is generally accepted that the social evil or prostitution is increased by the common ignorance of young people of both sexes regarding the physical and social relations of sex.

Of course, it is not true that all prostitution is due to ignorance, for it often involves enlightened men and women. However, there seems to be good reason for believing that large numbers of people of both sexes might be kept out of prostitution by very simple sex-instruction. Let us look for a moment at some facts concerning the relation of the ignorance of the women to their entrance into the underworld, and later consider certain reasons why many men patronize the social evil.

With regard to the women victims of prostitution, it seems to be generally accepted that economic pressure, feeble-mindedness, bad social environment, and unguided instincts, independently or combined, are the chief causes of their downfall. *Why women enter prostitution.* However, there is a deeper reason why numerous women enter prostitution, for all of these factors commonly operate because of inadequate sexual knowledge. In short, ignorance is the fundamental cause of much prostitution on the part of women. Many a girl with starvation wages, bad social surroundings, subnormal mentality, or even intense instincts is able to keep her womanhood because she knows the awful dangers of sexual promiscuity. For our present educational purposes, it is sufficient to point out the opinion of competent social workers that knowledge might often counteract the forces that lead women from virtue and down into prostitution.

A large number of men patronize prostitution because they are ignorant in one or more of the following respects. Some of them have drifted into abnormal sexual habits *Men also ignorant.* when they were boys, and later into illicit relations. Some of them did not know the effect of alcoholic drinks in leading many young men to their first immoral sexual acts. Some of them have deliberately patronized prostitution because they have accepted as truth the monstrous lie that sexual activity is necessary to preserve the health of men.[1] Most of the men do not realize that prostitution offers great danger to their own health, still greater danger to the health of innocent wives and children, and a greatly shortened life for many women who are the victims of sexual slavery. Most men do not know that dark tragedies are often concealed beneath the apparent gay life of the women who are victims of sexual degradation. These are some of the things of which many young men I have known were very ignorant, and it has been no difficult task to trace a close connection between their ignorance and their vice.

Looking at the social evil from any point of view, it seems to me that ignorance, dense ignorance, is largely responsible for the existence of that darkest blot on our boasted civilization — the social-sexual evil.

Ignorance the chief cause.

No matter how we look at the established facts regarding prostitution, they all point to the need of sexual instruction for the protection of the youth of both sexes. The Chicago Vice Commission concluded that "the lack of information, education and training with reference to the function and control of the sexual instinct, and the consequences of its abuse and perversion, appears at every point of

[1] See "The Sexual Necessity," by Drs. Howell and Keyes.

our inquiry for the sources of the supply of the victims of vice, either as the cause of the perversion of children and youth or as a complication of all other causes."[1] Of course, we dare not dream that any sex-instruction that now seems possible will completely eradicate prostitution; but we do know of thousands of boys and girls who have been directed to safety by knowledge of some fundamental sexual facts.

Concerning presentation of the social evil by fiction and the drama, there is much honest disagreement. My personal opinion is that little good is done by the theater or by such publications as Reginald Kaufmann's "House of Bondage," and Elizabeth Robin's "My Little Sister." They all leave the unsophisticated reader with an exaggerated and even hysterical notion that white slavery is exceedingly common and the main cause of prostitution. Certainly the great majority of the army of prostitutes, both public and clandestine, in America, and a still higher percentage on the continent of Europe, did not become novitiates of vice in prisons of prostitution. *Sex plays and novels.*

It seems to me that a very limited reading regarding the social evil is sufficient for one who is not engaged in medical or social work that requires scientific knowledge of this darkest side of human life. Certainly, the indiscriminate reading of vice investigations is dangerous for many young people, — for young *Limited reading desirable.*

[1] See also, Henderson's "Education with Reference to Sex."

men because some of them are allured into personal investigations, and for young women because they get an exaggerated and pessimistic view of all sexual problems. For the intelligent reader who wants the general information that every public-spirited citizen should have, the well-known book by Jane Addams will serve both as an outline and an encyclopedia of the social evil. Social workers and some educators will find use for the other books mentioned below.

Jane Addams. — "A New Conscience and an Ancient Evil." (Macmillan).
Seligman, E. R. A. (Editor). — "The Social Evil." (Putnam.) Contains bibliography on the subject.
Sumner, Dean W. T., and others. — "The Social Evil in Chicago." Vice-Commission Report, 1911. Now published by the American Social Hygiene Association. The "introduction and summary" (pp. 25–47) deserves careful reading.
Cocks, O. G. — "The Social Evil" (Association Press).

"Vigilance," a journal devoted to attacking the social evil, has been discontinued and replaced by bulletins of the American Social Hygiene Association, 105 West 40th Street, New York City.

§ 9. *The Fourth Problem for Sex-education: Illegitimacy*

Most awful of all the results of the sexual mistakes of men and women are the unmarried mothers and their illegitimate children. Of course, I know that there are well-meaning people who argue that motherhood is the supreme fact and that the formality of a marriage ceremony is merely a medievalism in our laws and customs;

Society condemns illegitimacy.

but the inexorable truth remains that our modern social system is centered around the home which is strictly regulated by church and state and public opinion.[1] Whatever may be the philosophical rights and wrongs of individual freedom in sexual relationship, the facts of practical life are that an overwhelming majority of the most intelligent people are united in support of our established laws and customs demanding legitimacy of motherhood and birthright. As a result of this age-old stand for legitimacy, illegitimate mothers and children do not have a square deal at the bar of public opinion. Everybody knows that the vast majority of illegitimate children do not have a fair chance in the world's work. Professor Cattell, in *Science*, March, 1914, points out that since illegitimates occur one in every twenty-five births in the United States, and since they are on the whole equal to other children in mentality, there ought to be forty of them among the thousand leading men of science designated in the directory of the "American Men of Science;" but none are known. The conclusion must be that illegitimate children do not have an equal chance at education which leads to prominence in science. But it is not simply a matter of limited education, for in every way the fate of most illegitimate children is usually pitiful. Only now and then one born under a lucky star is adopted and educated by large-minded foster parents who recognize that the

[1] See chapter on "Motherhood and Marriage" in Foerster's "Marriage and the Sex Problem."

illegitimate is not responsible for having come into this world under conditions opposed to the best interests of society.

It seems to be generally accepted that in the vast majority of cases, unmarried mothers and illegitimate children are due to ignorance of the women. Women who are professionally immoral do not bear many children.[1] In fact, excepting the feeble-minded prostitutes, the general rule is that those who are mothers have only one child and that one the result of the first sexual errors. It is a safe general conclusion that ignorance of sexual laws is responsible for the great majority of cases of illegitimacy.

Ignorance the cause.

Edith Livingston Smith, of Boston, in an article on "Unmarried Mothers" in *Harper's Weekly* for September 6, 1913, expressed views of the causes of illegitimacy that many a social worker will indorse heartily:

"I see shop girls and waitresses, factory girls and maids, chorus girls, stenographers, and governesses, each with a different story, each with the same terror of the consequences of their folly. 'I never knew,' they tell me, 'I never knew there were such temptations.' . . .

"Let us go back to the question of sex-education of the public. Silence has been the policy in the past. We have taught our children biology and natural history, we have taught them physiology, carefully

---

[1] As an illustration of this fact, out of 558 Pittsburgh professional prostitutes, 406 had never had children. Of the 152 who were mothers, only 24 had two or more children.

ignoring the organs of reproduction; we have warned the young to make use of their senses and their brains, but we have refused to recognize the very force that guides all these instincts, the vital power of sex. Yet, in the face of this stupidity, acknowledging the call of the age, girls are sent out into the industrial world, where they fight shoulder to shoulder with men. Here they find potential worth of their individualities; here they meet with the same — no, greater — temptation than their brothers, but with no knowledge to guide them, no traditions to give them poise, no ameliorating factor of social tenderness or tolerance when inexperience fails to temper their emotions and their femininity. . . .

"A girl's protection must come from without, a boy's from within. Every boy who reaches the age of adolescence knows his nature. It asserts itself. His sex instincts are dominant, aggressive. He is man, the father of the race, and the laws of procreation are to him an open book. A girl stays innocent until she is awakened. It is the kiss, the touch, the senses stirred, that make her, in the glory of her womanhood or in her shame, acknowledge her sex.

"The very frailty of such a girl, her dependence upon her intuitions and emotions, the triumph of feeling over intellect, place her in greater danger than her brothers, even were their responsibility to society the same. But, add to this the fact that in yielding to sexual temptation she has the burden of child-bearing — how much more necessary that she should have some knowledge of what she is to meet in the world, or what she must combat, lest her emotions forestall her intelligence as physical development precedes mental appreciation."

Illegitimacy is often due to ignorance of men as well as of women. Prominent physicians have cited from their notebooks cases of "protected" children in early adolescence who instinctively entered into sexual relationship in utter ignorance of the natural result. Such cases where the boy is entirely ignorant must be very rare; but there are probably many boys who do not really understand that the sexual act is very likely to lead to a ruined life for the girl companion and her offspring. Arthur Donnithorne, in "Adam Bede," did not forecast that his act would lead to the ruin of Hetty Sorrel and her condemnation for infanticide.

Men also ignorant.

It is obvious that something more than the ordinary biological facts of reproduction must be included in sex-instruction that tries to prevent such tragedies. In another lecture we shall consider moral teaching, but here let us look at the cold facts of life that ought to be taught at some appropriate time to young people. Not only should they know the simple biological probability that sexual relationship will lead to reproduction, but they should be led to consider the relentless consequences of illegitimate propagation. On this latter point general literature, *e.g.*, "Adam Bede" and "The Scarlet Letter," teaches some impressive lessons.

More than biology needed.

Another point needs emphasis with the numerous young people, especially men, who are not controlled by moral laws, who know the probabilities of illegitimacy occurring, but who have acquired the popular impression that the order of nature is easily changed. Many physicians and social workers know girls who have gone down because they were persuaded to trust the efficiency of popular ways and means of avoiding the natural outcome of the sexual act. Hence, young people of both sexes should somehow learn that under the conditions that usually attend illicit union there is always a strong probability that the ways of nature cannot be easily circumvented. It is unlawful to explain, except to medical audiences, why this is so; but much illegitimacy will be prevented if it can be made widely known among young men and women that, according to reliable physicians, tragedies of illegitimacy are often due to misplaced confidence in popular methods of contraception.

There is yet another line of information that if widely known might have some bearing on the problem of illicit sexual relations: Physicians and social workers report that many young men and some women know the possibility of illegitimate pregnancy, but feel safe because they know the addresses of doctors and midwives who will perform criminal operations. The great danger of the operation, especially at the hands of such third-class doctors as would attempt to terminate pregnancy criminally, should be widely known by the general public, which only now and then gets a hint in the newspaper reports of a tragedy involving some unfortunate girl. *Criminal operations.*

There is the widespread misunderstanding among young men that sexual hunger is as insistent in virtuous young women as in themselves and that therefore illicit gratification is a mutual gain and responsibility. Some young men may be guided by the information that there is much reliable evidence indicating that, while an innate tendency towards general emotions of affection is strong in the average young woman, there is general absence of the localized passions that naturally and automatically develop in young men. In other words, the first definite sexual temptation is likely to come to a young woman from outside herself, and young men should be impressed with their responsibility for allowing even the beginning of situations that may arouse dormant but dangerous instincts.

Relative passion of men and women.

§ 10. *The Fifth Problem for Sex-education: Sexual Morality*

In this lecture I shall set forth the proposition that a definitely organized scheme of education should aim directly at making young people strict adherents of the established code of sexual morality. For brevity, I shall occasionally speak of morality and immorality, omitting the qualifying word "sexual."

This lecture, in fact this entire series of lectures on sex-education, is based on the fundamental proposition that sexual morality demands that sexual union be restricted to monogamic marriage, and conversely, that such sexual relation outside of marriage is immoral. Such a definition of sexual morality is accepted by church and state and the chief citizens in every civilized country. It is the only practical definition which is satisfactory to the vast majority of educated American men and women, even to those who believe in freedom of divorce and in forgiveness for youthful transgressions of the accepted moral code. Sexual morality has had changeable standards, and in other times and countries custom has made polygamy and promiscuity acceptable as moral; but the monogamic ideal of morality now prevails in the world's best life.

Definition of sexual morality.

Monogamic morality as a protection for family life means much more in America than in Europe. It is true that there is an astounding amount of prostitution in America, but we should be grateful that our ideals of the monogamic family have not been seriously influenced and seem to be slowly but surely improving among our best people. As illustrations of our adherence to monogamic law, let me give some facts for comparison of America and continental Europe. In America, illegitimate births are not accurately reported but are probably less than five per cent of the total number for the whole country. Locally the proportion is often very much higher. Thus in Washington, D.C., where (1914) over ten thousand, chiefly negroes, live in alleys between

Morality in America and Europe.

the streets and under extremely unhygienic and immoral conditions, fifty per cent of the children are illegitimate, while but twenty per cent of the colored children born of mothers living outside the alleys, and less than eleven per cent of the total born of all races in the city are illegitimate. In various small American regions with a white population the proportion of illegitimacy is astoundingly high, but the average for the entire country is hopefully low. In many German towns statistics show above twenty-five per cent, and in the whole empire, more than half the legitimate first-born children are conceived before marriage. All writers, the German ones included, seem to agree that the majority of Teutonic men and women enter into free unions before marriage and public opinion does not severely condemn.

In many rural districts of England, France, and Sweden, and even in London and Paris, a large percentage of the marriages are simply legalization of free unions. In short, in all these countries the monogamic ideal is not followed by a large percentage of people. It must be remembered that the great majority of people involved in the above figures are of the peasant and laboring classes; conditions are quite different among women of the educated classes. These must ultimately set the moral standards for the masses.

Our American conditions are quite different, especially outside of the large cosmopolitan cities. It is impossible not to believe in the moral integrity of the great majority of unmarried women in

America. Certainly even in our worst communities we have no such general immorality of women as above European figures suggest. Perhaps wholesale prostitution in which one public woman may be the mistress of ten, twenty, or even fifty men, may tend to protect any equal number of American women; whereas in Europe a peasant woman would probably be for a time the paramour of one man, thus tending to make equal numbers of immoral men and women.

However, it matters nothing for our present purposes what may be the explanation of conditions of sexual promiscuity here or abroad. The one great fact is that our national code of morality is a monogamic one, approved as ideal even by many of those who fail to live strictly in harmony with its dictates. Hence, all Americans who are prominently interested in sex-education believe that it should aim to make our young people more ready to accept and understand morality according to the monogamic ideal.

Those who are interested in this problem of morality as related to marriage should read Foerster's "Marriage and the Sex Problem."

Among those who see the need of teaching sex-ethics as a part of the larger outlook of sex-education, there are two points of view: (1) those who favor the teaching of sex-ethics with the hope of preventing the hygienic problems arising from immorality, and (2) those who believe in sexual morality for its own sake or as an accepted code of conduct.

Relation of sex-hygiene and ethics.

The founders of the American Society for Sanitary and Moral Prophylaxis placed sanitation first in the name and stated in the constitution that "the object of this Society is to limit the spread of diseases which have their origin in the Social Evil. It proposes to study every means, sanitary, moral, and administrative, which promise to be most effective for this purpose." Most of the papers that have been read at the meetings of the Society have emphasized the sanitary aim as primary, and the moral aim as a means to the hygienic end; but in the past three years there has been a decided tendency towards placing emphasis upon morality, and recently the executive committee of the Society voted to propose the following revised statement: "The aim of this Society is to promote the appreciation of the sacredness of human sexual relation, and thereby to minimize the moral and physical evils resulting from ignorance and vice." This change of emphasis is well expressed in President Keyes's report to the Society (*Journal*, Vol. V, No. 1).

As to the relation between sex-hygiene and sex-ethics as phases of the larger sex-education, there has been much discussion. Several writers have contended that there is some conflict between sanitary and moral ends, but have failed to convince most readers that hygiene and ethics should not be associated in teaching. In fact, the most impressive sex-hygiene is that relating to social disease, and its value is chiefly in the ethical appeal for protection of innocent wives and children.

Most prominent of those who have declared that hygienic and moral teaching should be dissociated is Dr. Richard C. Cabot, of Boston. I shall discuss his point of view in connection with a later lecture on "Criticisms of Sex-education" (§ 46). In the present discussion of sexual morality as an important reason for sex-education, it is sufficient to say that Dr. Cabot seems to disagree with other teachers on the question of the influence of formal instruction on the morals of people. {Dr. Cabot's view.}

Sex-education is now commonly understood to be attempting to solve the moral as well as the hygienic problems of sex. As suggested before, these two lines of problems are clearly related but not coincident; for sexual health and morals are not entirely coördinated. {Moral and hygienic problems.} We must not overlook the possibility that the marvellous progress of bacteriological and medical science may some day largely reduce the health problems of sex without improving morality. In fact, sexual immorality that is hygienic does actually exist to a limited extent. Such facts indicate that while sex-education was first planned to solve health problems, the ultimate sex-education must attempt to guide sexual conduct by moral principles. This coming need of more emphasis on the moral problems of sex should be clearly foreseen by those who are interested in sex-education.

Now, while sexual morality as commonly understood is a direct aim of sex-education, it is not, in the opinion of many people, the ideal and ultimate goal of sex-education in its broadest outlook.

Super-morality desirable. There is something higher than conventional morality for the reason that, while natural sexual union in monogamic marriage is never legally or ecclesiastically immoral, it is very often far from ideal. It is not ideal if it is unethical, unhygienic, or unæsthetic. It is unethical, if it is not a bi-personal desideratum (*i.e.*, based on mutual love[1]); it is unhygienic when not promotive and conservative of health; and it is unæsthetic if the concomitant psychical reactions are not in harmony with the beautiful in nature and life. In all these ways, morality as commonly and legally and ecclesiastically understood may fall very far short of the ideal sexual relationships. Such an ideal is now held by many men and women who wish that morality might mean to all the world not simply the limitation of sexual union to monogamic marriage, but also that it might be made to mean an all-satisfying monogamic affection and comradeship based on certain physiological, psychical, æsthetic, and ethical laws that underlie human sexual potentialities. Such would be a morality so

---

[1] Many thinking men and women now agree with Ellen Key that "marriage is immoral without mutual love," that "love is the sole decisive point of view in questions concerning this relationship," that "it will come to pass that no finely sensitive woman will become a mother except through mutual love," that "everything which is exchanged between husband and wife in their life together can only be the free gift of love, can never be demanded by one or the other as a right." (Key — "The Morality of Woman.")

far beyond the accepted standards that for convenience we may call it super-morality, or the new morality. This, I sincerely believe, is the ultimate goal of sex-education in its largest outlook.

Among those who have contributed to the sex-education movement there are none who have properly emphasized this super-morality, which, I believe, is the ultimate goal of the larger sex-education for the most enlightened people. The definition that sex-education means all instruction which aims to help young people prepare to solve for themselves the sexual problems that inevitably come to every normal individual, is broad enough to include all questions of hygiene, morality, and super-morality that may come into one's life. The third aim of sex-education (§ 16) which refers to the "social, ethical, and psychical aspects of sex as affecting the individual life in relation to other individuals," should be understood as meaning first a stand for morality and then, this having been attained, super-morality is an easy stage forward. The same idea was touched by the writer in a paper on "Biology in Sex-Instruction" (*Journal of Society of Sanitary and Moral Prophylaxis*, October, 1911) in these words: "If the great questions of sex relationship are ever satisfactorily solved, it must be through the direct application of the four sciences which are centered around human life, namely, psychology, ethics, sociology, and last, but far from least, æsthetics. As we have seen, biology teaches much

Super-morality deserves emphasis.

directly bearing on the purely physical aspects of the perpetuation of human life, and its study is absolutely necessary for mental attitude and basal facts; but the keystone of the arch of sex-education must be contributed by these four sciences which touch human life much deeper than the merely physical, to which the science of biology is limited. Above all we must look to these sciences for the solution of the problems of sex in relation to society, which more than any physical ills have led to our present problems concerning sexual disharmonies."

But while there is something attractive in this larger interpretation of sex-education as looking forward to the highest adaptation of sex and life, I realize that as a practical matter we must first of all work with young people for sexual morality as defined by the accepted code. We must remember that the vast majority of people are not yet ready, and will not soon be ready, for a code of super-morality. Confusion might result from an attempt at wholesale teaching of such idealism of sex relationship. Certainly, so far as sex-education aims to help immature young people, there is nothing to do but hold up monogamic marriage as the basis of our accepted morality; but the higher view of super-morality should be promulgated as rapidly as possible among people who are advanced enough to understand that morality as defined by church and state is not the best interpretation of life's possibilities. To many it is a significant fact

Super-morality not for the masses.

that we now find numerous young men and women ready to stand for super-morality as a foundation for monogamic marriage. Fortunately, such individuals need not wait for the world to grasp the idea of super-morals; and already there is many a home in which the higher view of life and sex prevails.

Immorality in sexual lines should not be overstressed when teaching young people. Rather should there be emphasis on the moral, the normal, the healthful, the helpful, and the æsthetic processes in human life. We should emphasize sexual health and morals, not disease and immorality. *Cautious teaching concerning immorality.* Concerning immoral living in general, young people should know only enough for necessary warning. Curiosity derived from extensive knowledge of immorality has drawn many a young man into the whirlpool of sexual depravity. It is beyond question that in sexual lines there is the danger that Pope saw when he declared that vice is a monster that seen too oft, we first endure, then pity, then embrace. Sex-education should guard against such dangerous familiarity with vice.

§ 11. *The Sixth Problem for Sex-education: Sexual Vulgarity*

Even a limited study of the prevailing attitude towards sex and reproduction convinces one that back of the greatest sexual problems of our times is the almost universal secrecy, disrespect, vulgarity, and irreverence concerning every aspect of sex and reproduction. *Present attitude.*

Even expectant motherhood is commonly concealed as long as possible, and all reference to the developing new life is usually accompanied with blushes and tones suggestive of some great shame. Nothing sexual is commonly regarded as sacred. Love and marriage, motherhood and birth, are all freely selected as themes for sexual jests, many of them so vulgar that no printed dictionary supplies the necessary words. And I am not simply referring to the great masses of uneducated people, for the saddest fact is that a very large proportion of intelligent people have not an open-minded and respectful attitude concerning sex and reproduction.

Now, unless we can devise some way to counteract the prevailing narrow, vulgar, disrespectful, and irreverent attitude towards all aspects of sex and reproduction; unless we can make people see sexual processes in all their normal aspects as noble, beautiful, and splendid steps in the great plan of nature; unless we can substitute a philosophical and æsthetic view of sex relationship for the time-worn interpretation of everything sexual as inherently vulgar, base, ignoble, and demanding asceticism for those who would reach the highest spiritual development; unless we can begin to make these changes in the prevailing attitude towards sex and reproduction, we cannot make any decided advance in the attempt to help solve sexual problems by special instruction.

Vast change of attitude needed.

First of all, sex-education must work for a purified and dignified attitude which sees vulgarity and impurity only when the functions of sex have been voluntarily and knowingly misused and thereby debased. Sex-education must work against the idea that sexual processes are inherently vulgar, degraded, base, and impure. Such an interpretation is correct only when sexual instincts are uncontrolled and thereby out of harmony with the highest ideals of life. But control does not mean asceticism which aims at complete subjugation of sexual instincts and would annihilate them if that were biologically possible. The early Christians, disgusted with the sexual degradation of the paganistic and materialistic Romans, preached a doctrine of sexual asceticism as the ideal for those who would rise to the heights of spiritual life. This pessimistic interpretation of the relation of sex and life has persisted even in some ecclesiastical teachings of the twentieth century, and probably has had not a little responsibility for the widely accepted and depressing view that sex is a necessary but regrettable fact of human life.

Fortunately, the old ascetic point of view is passing rapidly. Nineteenth-century science has given us a nobler view of the physical Attitude world. Scientifically considered, matter changing. is no longer base and degraded. Especially has the biological science of the past fifty years made *living* matter and its activities profoundly impressive. And of the life-activities none are so significant and so all-important as those relating to the perpetuation of the human species. Biological science has taught this emphatically, and the processes connected with sex have been lifted to a place of dignity and purity.

The old asceticism, with its uniformly dark outlook on life, has no lessons worth while in our modern problems relating to sex.[1] We need severe control and not annihilation of our most powerful instincts. The bright outlook of æsthetics rather than the dark one of asceticism should prevail, for sex-instincts and processes are essentially pure and beautiful phases of that wonderful something we call "life." Sex-education should aim to give this attitude by presenting life as fundamentally free from the degradation arising from misuse and misunderstanding of sex.

Æsthetic attitude desirable.

The æsthetic interpretation of sex is no new ideal. Canon Lyttleton, formerly Head Master of Eton College and later Canon of Westminster, believed that "viewed rightly, the subject of sex, the ever-recurring miracle of generation and birth, is full of nobleness, purity, and health." The late Dr. Prince A. Morrow wrote, "the sex function is intimately connected with the physical, mental, and moral development. Its right

Not a new ideal.

---

[1] Foerster, in his "Marriage and the Sex Problem," urges that self-control over sexual passions is the working of the old idea of asceticism, which he believes "should be regarded, not as a negation of nature nor as an attempt to extirpate natural forces, but as practice in the art of self-discipline. Its object should be to show humanity what the human will is capable of performing, to serve as an encouraging example of the conquest of the spirit over the animal self." My personal view is that nothing is gained by confusing self-control and the old asceticism.

use is the surest basis of individual health, happiness and usefulness in life, as well as of racial permanence and prosperity. Its abuse and misuse is the cause of a vast deal of disease and misery." And finally, we may quote President-Emeritus Eliot of Harvard University: "Society must be relieved by sound instruction of the horrible doctrine that the begetting and bearing of children are in the slightest degree sinful or foul processes. That doctrine lies at the root of the feeling of shame in connection with these processes and of the desire for secrecy. The plain fact is that there is nothing so sacred and propitious on earth as the bringing of another normal child into the world in marriage. There is nothing staining or defiling about it, and therefore there is no need for shame or secrecy, but only for pride and joy. This doctrine should be part of the instruction given to all young people."

If sex-education succeeds in giving young people this enlightened attitude, there will be little difficulty in solving most of the ethical and hygienic problems of sex. A young man who has caught a glimpse of the highest interpretation of sex in its relation to human life, in short a young man to whom all natural sexual processes are essentially pure and noble and beautiful, is not one who will make grave hygienic mistakes in his own life, and he will not be personally connected with the social evil and its diseases, and he will avoid almost intuitively the physiologic and psychologic mistakes that most

Attitude all-important in sex-education.

often cause matrimonial disaster. Everything, then, in successful sex-education depends upon the attitude formed in the minds of learners; and towards this our major efforts should be directed.

The prevailing vulgar attitude towards sex will not be greatly improved by repeated emphasis upon the animal nature of reproduction in attempts at supporting the thesis that propagation is the sole function of sexual processes in human life. Such an interpretation of human sexuality as purely animalistic in function is implied, if not expressed, by some workers for the "purity" movement. I sincerely believe that such a view will inevitably tend to increase the feeling that sexual processes are heritages from the beasts which unfortunately must be tolerated because nature has provided no other way for perpetuating human life.

Comparison with animals not helpful.

An intelligent woman, a happy wife and mother, who had accepted this ascetic and pessimistic view of sex, said the other day: "Oh, love and marriage and motherhood would be so beautiful were it possible to escape the unspeakably vulgar facts of physical life!" Poor woman! It must have been some fiend incarnate who in the guise of a prophet of purity preached to her the animalistic interpretation of sex, which made her overlook the fact that the very beauty which she could not quite grasp ·had its origin in her emotions arising from the despised sexual nature.

Sexual pessimism.

This is not an isolated case. Several young women who have graduated from college within ten years vouch for the statement that many thoughtful students are strong in the belief that ideal marriage is platonic friendship and that it is a sad fact of life that husband and wife must lay aside their high ideals in order to become parents.

Such depressing interpretations of life are bound to come from the radical type of "purity" preaching based on the sexual mistakes of the past and on the lives of animals. A similar pessimistic view regarding the function of eating might be based on mistakes of drunkards and gluttons and on the habits of the porcine family. If these are to guide our conduct, then food-taking is to be regarded as a necessary but vulgar habit inherited from our animal ancestors; and if we are to be logical and attempt to rise to ideal purity in eating, we must hasten to dispense with the culinary science and all the æsthetics which have made civilized eating a fine art. Of course, this is just what the strict ascetic does; but such radical disbelievers in the pleasures that we have associated with eating would be declared lunatics in any civilized country.

I have chosen eating for illustrating my point, for the demands for food and for sexual activity are the two primal and necessary forms of hunger. The hunger for food has led to the refinements of civilized dining, but there has been great evolution. The animals feed (German, fressen) in order to satisfy hunger only; civilized

Two kinds of hunger.

humans eat (essen) not only to satisfy the hunger appetite inherited from the animals, but also for the sake of the concomitant social æsthetic pleasures that add much to the joy of living. Now, if we are logical, we must interpret on parallel lines the sexual hunger that is necessary for the perpetuation of human life. Like eating, it is a necessary function inherited from the animals; but there has been an evolution of greater significance. In the animal world, sexual activity has only one function, reproduction; but human life at its highest has superadded psychical and social meaning to sexual relationships, and the result has been affection and the human family. If we reject this higher view of the double significance of sexuality in human life, and insist that only the necessary propagative function is worthy of recognition, it is almost inevitable that most people will continue to accept the hopeless view that human sexuality is on the same vulgar plane as that of the animals; in short, that it is only an animal function. This, I insist, is a depressing interpretation that will never help overcome the prevailing vulgar attitude toward sex.

It is only by frankly recognizing and developing the psychical and æsthetic meanings that are dis-

Human sexuality more than animal. tinctly human and superadded to the merely propagative function of the animals, that people can be led far away from the vulgar outlook on sex and reproduction in human life.

There is no question that wholesome attitude towards sex and reproduction is closely associated with the problems of sexual morality, and especially so far as educational procedure is concerned. It is true that large numbers of moral people hold the vulgar attitude towards sex and reproduction; but for people who do not accept the moral code without question there is probably no better way of teaching sexual morality than by influencing the individual's attitude. There are many people who stand for sexual morality for no other reason than that they have a dignified and æsthetic attitude towards sex. *Relation of attitude and morality.*

There is much evidence that the world is rapidly improving in this respect. Sexual vulgarity seems to represent a stage in the evolution of human life from the barbaric to the fully civilized. The sexual vulgarity of primitive peoples, both ancient and modern, has been all too frequently recalled by writers whose pseudo-scientific superficiality leads them to believe that knowledge concerning barbaric and ultra-bestial sensuality will help solve modern sex problems. In the classical days when Venus and Bacchus and other deities of sensuality were worshipped by their devotees, there was sexual vulgarity in action and language such as now exists only among the most ignorant or depraved people in civilized lands. The advent of Christian civilization in Europe left no place for temples and worship of sensuality, but still the age-old tendency towards *Sexual vulgarity a stage in evolution.*

a crude and barbaric kind of sexual vulgarity and obscenity has continued in folklore, in colloquial language, and in literature. However, there has been a vast change in the attitude of the best people within the last two centuries. Once many English writers, many of them now deservedly obscure, published prose and poetry that would now be criminal. An unexpurgated edition of Shakespeare's "Complete Works," or of Boccaccio's "Decameron," could not be circulated through the United States mails, and there are many good people who are asking how long we shall continue to allow the unexpurgated "Old Testament" the privilege of circulation. It is not simply prose and poetry that has been purified. Scientific literature has shown the influence of the reaction against obscenity. Linnæus and other naturalists of the past were fond of giving scientific names that perpetuated vulgar comparisons with sexual organs, but no naturalist of the present day would dare suggest such designations for unnamed animals and plants. The older medical literature contains abundant obscenities; but scientific dignity, as well as the refinement of modern medical writers, has tended to compel the elimination of vulgarity. However, there are still too many physicians, especially those working with venereal and genito-urinary diseases, who go out of their way to illuminate their conversations, lectures, books, and magazine articles with veiled vulgarity. Even high-class medical journals occasionally contain illustrations of this tendency. However, the medical profession as a class stands for dignified scientific presentation of facts, and obscenity will soon be tabooed in medical and all other reputable literature. Save for occasional emanations privately printed by and for degenerate persons, public obscenity will soon be unknown. Its complete disappearance will have a vast influence upon the problem of sexual attitude.

§ 12. *The Seventh Problem for Sex-instruction: Marriage*

It is the consensus of opinion of numerous physicians, ministers, and lawyers that a very large proportion of matrimonial disharmonies have their foundation in the common misunderstanding of the physiology and especially of the psychology of sex. In the opinion of many students of sexual problems, this is the strongest reason for sex-instruction. It is certainly a line in which limited spread of information has already given some definite and satisfactory results. Many of my friends and former students have helped me accumulate a long list of cases in which scientific knowledge regarding sex has prevented and corrected matrimonial disagreements; and having easily found so much definite influence of sex-science upon marriage, I am forced to believe that sex-instruction specially organized for people of marriageable age is already giving results of tremendous importance to very many individuals. Large numbers of young people are

Physiology and psychology of marriage.

already awake to the need of scientific guidance in marriage, and there is a great demand for helpful information.

Advanced sex-instruction with reference to the problems of marriage need not wait for general establishment of elementary instruction for children of school ages. Lectures and books are already reaching large numbers of adults. Such enlightenment will help in two ways, by the influence on marriage and by preparing adults to teach children.

There is another side to the problem of marriage that points to need of the larger sex-education. **Other knowledge needed.** Physiology and psychology of sex are fundamental; but they alone are not sufficient to complete that mutual adjustment and understanding which marriage at the full development of its possibilities involves. Matrimonial harmony cannot be entirely a problem of applied science, as some superficial devotees of science seem to think; for science can never analyze those subtle and ever-varying qualities that go to make up what we call personality, and marriage in its largest outlook is the intimate blending of two personalities. Psychological and physiological knowledge will undoubtedly help the two married individuals in their progress towards the harmonious adjustment of their individualities; but there are many little, but often serious, problems that the physiology and psychology of sex cannot solve. They are problems that involve mutual affection, comradeship, sympathy, unselfishness, coöperation, kindliness, and devotion of husband and wife. Obviously, these can never be developed by any formal instruction.

Probably there is no better way to help young people realize the possibilities of matrimonial harmony than by suggesting wholesome litera- **Helpful** ture. Some of this is a part of the world's **literature.** general treasure of books that in prose and poetry, in history and romance, hold up a high ideal of love with marriage. There is much such literature that gives young people inspiration, but too much of it, like college life, ends with a commencement. "And then they were married and lived happily ever after" — is the familiar closing as the novelist rings down the curtain after reciting only the prologue in the life drama of his two lovers. We need more literature that does not end with the wedding march, but which gives young people the successful solution of the problems after marriage. Some such is available in history and biography; some in essays. As I write there come to my mind several books that have impressed me: Professor Palmer's "Life of Alice Freeman Palmer"; Leonard Huxley's "Life and Letters of T. H. Huxley," which gives many intimate glimpses of the ideal home life which the great biologist centered around Mrs. Huxley; William George Jordan's "Little Problems of Married Life"; Orrin Cock's "Engagement and Marriage"; and that much misunderstood [1] but helpful book

[1] Misunderstood, it seems to me, because her philosophy demanding that marriage begin with, exist with, and end with love means

"Love and Marriage" by Ellen Key. Many of the stories by Virginia Terhune Van de Water, published in the magazines and collected in a book entitled "Why I Left my Husband" (Moffatt, Yard), deal with real problems of married life.

The problems of co-education and coördinate education have not a little bearing on the adjustment of the two sexes in marriage. In these days when vocational education is fashionable in theory and is attracting attention in practice, we are told that co-education and coördinate education are mistakes because they provide the same training for both sexes. We are told that girls must be educated for their vocation of home-making, while boys must be educated for business, trades, or professions. Everywhere in this current movement for vocational education we find the emphasis placed on making education for the two sexes just as dissimilar as possible. Fortunately for the educational adjustments of the two sexes to each other, much of the present-day discussion that demands extensive sex specialization of education cannot be made practical and the training of the two sexes will inevitably continue to be quite similar, with at most a limited amount of time spent on application of certain knowledge to practical

Similar education of the sexes.

freedom in love, and this has been misinterpreted as "free love" in the sense of promiscuity. I know of no writer who stands for marriage on a higher plane than that advocated by Ellen Key. Her lecture on "Morality of Woman" (Seymour Co., Chicago) is a good condensed statement of her largest ideas and a helpful introduction to "Love and Marriage."

ends that are chiefly of interest to one sex only. By far the greater part of education from kindergarten through the university is in the nature of the fundamentals of knowledge and will continue to be essentially similar for both sexes. For illustration, the writer happens to be connected with a college which offers a four-year course and graduate work specially arranged with reference to household arts. Surely here is an opportunity for education far different from that of the typical college for men. As a matter of fact, there is great similarity. The greater part of the four years is filled with general courses in English, modern languages, chemistry, biology, physics, sociology, economics, and fine arts, while a minor part of the curriculum consists of courses in cookery, clothing, and household administration. The general courses are in essentials not different from courses in colleges for men. Here and there instructors select materials and in other ways relate the general courses to household arts, but after all a girl who completes these courses has acquired the same educational fundamentals that her brother gets in Columbia College or in any other standard college for men. It is only, then, in the cookery, clothing, and administration that there is sex-differentiated education, and even in these the practice necessary to acquire proficiency in technique is the chief peculiarity. So far as fundamental knowledge is concerned, cookery is chiefly an application of chemistry, physics, and physiology that could easily be made clear to one who had completed courses in these sciences in a college for men; dress design is an application of fine arts and its construction is a mechanical problem. The mental problems involved in dress design and making cannot be far different from house design and construction which are supposed to be primarily adapted to men.

On the whole, then, there is really little possibility of sex-differentiated education. This, I insist, is a **Little differentiation.** fortunate fact of vast importance in the mutual adjustment of the two sexes in marriage. There could be no adjustment on an intelligent basis if education could be utterly dissimilar. There can be perfect adjustment only when the two individuals are adjusted harmoniously, and that means similar outlooks on life's problems.

Many of the problems of the modern feministic movement are such as to demand rational education **Need of sex-education for feminism.** of both women and men with reference to sex and marriage. Let me quote C. Gasquoine Hartley, whose suggestive Chapters VIII and IX in her "Truth About Woman" (Dodd, Mead) deserve to live long after the readable but unscientifically applied earlier chapters are consigned to oblivion:

"To hear many women talk it would appear that the new ideal is a one-sexed world. A great army of women have espoused the task of raising their sex out of subjection. For such a duty the strength and energy of passion is required. Can this task be performed if the woman to any extent indulges in sex — otherwise subjection to man? Sexuality debases, even reproduction and birth are regarded as 'nauseating.' Woman is not free, only because she has been the slave to the primitive cycle of emotions which belong to physical love. The renunciation, the conquest of sex — it is this that must be gained. As for man, he has been shown up, women have found him out; his long-worn garments of authority and his mystery and glamour have been torn into shreds — woman will have none of him.

"Now obviously these are over-statements, yet they are the logical outcome of much of the talk that one hears. It is the visible sign of our incoherence and error, and in the measure of these follies we are sent back to seek the truth. Women need a robuster courage in the face of love, a greater faith in their womanhood, and in the scheme of Life. Nothing can be gained from the child's folly in breaking the toys that have momentarily ceased to please. The misogamist type of woman cannot fail to prove as futile as the misogamist man. Not 'Free *from* man' is the watch-cry of women's emancipation that surely is to be, but 'Free *with* man.'"

And further on the same author, considering the problem of the women of the common type that are classified as a "third sex," that of temperamental neuter, says:

"Economic conditions are compelling women to enter with men into the fierce competition of our disordered social state. Partly due to this reason, though much more, as I think, to the strong stirring in woman of her newly-discovered self, there has arisen what I should like to call an over-emphasized Intellectu-

Sex and intellectualism.

alism. Where sex is ignored there is bound to lurk danger. Every one recognizes the significance of the advance in particular cases of women towards a higher intellectual individuation, and the social utility of those women who have been truly the pioneers of the new freedom; but this does not lessen at all the disastrous influence of an ideal which holds up the renunciation of the natural rights of love and activities of women, and thus involves an irreparable loss to the race by the barrenness of many of its finest types. The significance of such Intellectuals must be limited, because for them the possibility of transmission by inheritance of their valuable qualities is cut off, and hence the way is closed to a further progress. And, thus, we are brought back to that simple truth from which we started; there are two sexes, the female and the male, on their specific differences and resemblances blended together in union every true advance in progress depends — on the perfected woman and the perfected man."

One who studies carefully the various aspects of the extreme feministic movement must admit that there are many signs of the dangers which the above quotations point out so clearly. Of course, we cannot believe in the sincerity of all of the numerous women of thirty-five to fifty years who pretend to ignore sex completely. Probably most of them have discovered that they have misunderstood themselves; but it is also probable that they have discovered too late for making a readjustment in their own lives. However, it matters little whether such women have really succeeded in ignoring sex. The

Young women misled by sexual pessimists.

real problem for educational attack lies in the fact that such women often succeed in proselyting young women under twenty-five, and these in turn may not come to see the real truth about sex and life until ten or fifteen years later. Clearly, organized education must protect young women against such influences.

The greatest good which may come from the sex-education movement is not prevention or elimination of social diseases, it is not improved health, it is not general acceptance of the moral law of sex, it is not one or all these that are devoutly to be hoped for; but far greater than such possible results from sex-education, it will bring to many a man and woman a deeper, nobler, and purer knowledge of what sex means for the coming race and of what it means now to each individual who realizes life's fullest possibilities in conjugal affection which culminates in new life and new motives for more affection. Such an understanding of sex in relation to home life will help this old world more than anything else which sex-education may accomplish. *(The greatest good in sex-education.)*

The problems of sex and marriage deserve far more attention than can be given in this lecture. I am convinced that knowledge of sex in its physical, psychical, social, and æsthetic aspects is the only sure foundation for harmonious marriage under modern conditions. Therefore, I believe this to be the greatest sex problem open to educational attack. *(The greatest sex problem.)*

86 SEX-EDUCATION

§ 13. *The Eighth Problem for Sex-instruction: Eugenics*

Eugenics, or the science of human good breeding, is just now the most popular of the problems concerning human sex and reproduction. In recent years, the biological investigators of heredity have published some startling facts which show that the human race must soon check its reckless propagation of the unfit and encourage reproduction by the best types of men and women. This is not the place for a review of the eugenic propositions. Those interested will find them in non-technical form in many books (see the bibliographical chapter of this book, page 248).

Meaning of eugenics.

Some of the chief facts of eugenics should be a part of every well-organized scheme of sex-instruction, and taught through biology (§ 17). Probably no other topic in biology is so likely to make an ethical-social appeal, for the central point of eugenics is the responsibility of the individual whose uncontrolled sexual actions may transmit undesirable and heritable qualities and bring a train of disaster to generations of descendants.

Eugenics in biology.

At this point we digress to correct the widespread error in confusing sex-hygiene and eugenics. Many people who ought to know better use the two terms synonymously, perhaps because they are afraid of that comparatively novel but frank prefix in "sex-hygiene." The fact is that eugenics and sex-hygiene have little in common. Eugenics is the

Relation of eugenics and sex-hygiene.

science of reproducing better humans by applying the established laws of genetics or heredity. In brief, it means, on the positive side, selecting desirable people as parents; and, negatively, preventing propagation by the undesirables. This is the sum total of the task of eugenics in the accurate sense of the term.

So far as we know, each coming generation will inherit only qualities that the parents inherited from their parents. It is a well-known principle of biology that changes in the bodies of human beings during their lifetime (dating from the fertilized egg that produces the individual) are never in any noticeable degree inherited by descendants. In short, acquired characteristics of the body tissues do not influence the germ plasm, the living matter concerned with heredity and reproduction, but the germ plasm that determines what the next generation will inherit is fixed at birth. Thus tuberculosis, alcoholism, gonorrhea, and syphilis may be acquired during the life of an individual, but do not become fixed in the germ plasm. If the infants show effects of any of these diseases, it is not because of true heredity but because they were infected or influenced before birth. Rarely does this happen to children of a tuberculous mother, but often to those of a syphilitic mother. In a gonorrheal ophthalmia neonatorum (specific inflammation of infants' eyes) it is a case of infection *during* birth.

Thus, it appears that sex-hygiene either personal or social (concerned with venereal diseases) is not a part of eugenics. It is, however, a phase of euthenics, which deals with the environmental factors that affect the individual life. It is clear, then, that sex-hygiene (in the strict medical sense) and eugenics are parallel and not conflicting. Eugenics aims to select better parents who will transmit their own qualities genetically. Sex-hygiene in its personal and social aspects will make healthier parents able to give their offspring a healthier start in life, especially because the offspring is free from the prenatal effects of disease.

Sex-hygiene and eugenics parallel.

The teaching of heredity and eugenics is intended to develop a sense of individual responsibility for the transmission of one's good or bad inherited qualities to offspring. The teaching of sex-hygiene, either personal or social, looks towards improving personal health and preventing infection and injurious influence on the unborn next generation. Obviously, we need both sex-hygiene and eugenics as part of the larger sex-instruction.

§ 14. *Summary of Lectures on Sex Problems*

We have made a general survey of the problems that offer reasons for sex-instruction. We have noted that some of the problems are concerned with health and, hence, lie within the scope of sex-hygiene in the strict sense of that term; but some of them have only the remotest relation to health and hygiene. On the contrary, they relate to the ethi-

Problems of health, attitude, and morals.

cal, social, and æsthetic attitude of individuals towards sex and reproduction. Obviously, these touch problems not of sex health, but of sex morality. In their educational importance I believe them as great, perhaps even greater, than those of sex-hygiene. In fact, I have come to believe that many individuals can best solve all their own sexual problems on the basis of moral and æsthetic attitude.

Considering, as we have done, the sex problems in their many aspects, we are forced to the conclusion that sex-education will prove adequate only when it combines instruction from the several points of view. It must be much more than the sex-hygiene with which the sex-instruction movement started. We need sexual knowledge that will conserve health, that will develop social and ethical and eugenic responsibility for sexual actions, that will lead to increased happiness as well as to improved health, and that will give a nobler and purer view of life's possibilities. In all these lines in which sex influences human life profoundly, sex-education holds out the hope of help towards a better life for all who receive and apply its lessons.

Many-sided instruction needed.

III

ORGANIZATION OF EDUCATIONAL ATTACK ON THE SEX PROBLEMS

§ 15. *The Task of Sex-education*

In the preceding series of lectures we have surveyed eight important sex problems that can never be solved, even in part, unless by wide-spread information that specifically guides the individual and organized society in the adjustment of sexual instincts to the peculiar conditions that obtain in our modern civilized life. To spread the knowledge that will help civilized humanity on towards the best possible adjustment of sex and life, and therefore to a pragmatic solution of sexual problems, is the task or the chief aim of sex-education.[1]

Pragmatic solution of sex problems.

Of course, only the ultra-Utopian dreamer claims that sex-education can solve all the sexual problems of civilized life, but even the most pessimistic disbeliever in the new movement admits that knowledge of sexual life will be helpful to the great majority of people. Hence, it is worth while to organize the educational attack

No hope for complete solution.

---

[1] To avoid misunderstanding, let me repeat from the first lecture that I am constantly thinking of sex-education in the larger sense; and instruction in schools can be, at best, only a part.

on the sex problems which we have considered in the preceding lectures. It seems to me that we may gain an advantage by frankly admitting that the educational attack is not expected to solve all sex problems for all people, for by such admission we put to flight those shallow cynics who have opposed the sex-education movement because they think (and probably correctly) that immorality and social diseases and all other sexual disharmonies will continue to exist as long as the human species does. Likewise, there will be dishonesty and murder and preventable diseases and all other human troubles in spite of education; but the advancement of learning has slowly and progressively reduced the sum total of all the disharmonies of life until now civilized people are largely free from many of the original or barbaric conditions. Along similar lines we may confidently think of sex-education as making a constantly advancing and victorious attack on the problems of life that have grown out of our primitive sexual instincts. Sex-education, like all other education, strives towards ideals that individuals and society may always approach but may never reach. It is only another case of Emerson's advice, "hitch your wagon to a star," which means the adoption of high ideals that lead ever on and on towards better life. *Constant advance towards ideals.*

With this understanding that *the task of sex-education is the ever-advancing improvement of sexual conditions in individual as well as in social life,* let us turn now to consider the possible lines for definite educational attack on the chief problems of sex. It will be most helpful if we first analyze the general task of sex-education into some specific aims that may definitely guide instruction, and then in later lectures consider the methods and detailed subject matter of sex-instruction.

§ 16. *The Aims of Sex-education*

Since the revelations concerning the disastrous physical effects of sexual immorality, especially as it exists in the commercialized conditions of the social evil, have had the chief influence in awakening intelligent people from their age-long ignorance and indifference concerning the great sex problems, it was natural that those who first proposed special instruction should have emphasized the social evil and its diseases so much as to create the widespread but erroneous impression that the great aim of sex-education is to teach the distressing facts concerning the pathological consequences of immorality.

Emphasis on social disease.

Now, without in the least underestimating the vast importance of the emphasis placed on sexual immorality and social diseases in the splendid pioneer work of the late Dr. Morrow and others for the sex-education movement, and without suggesting that these topics should be neglected while reorganizing the educational attack on sex problems, I believe that so far as formal instruction in homes, schools, and col-

Other problems need emphasis.

leges is concerned, we may gain a decided advantage if we now recognize and declare boldly that the physical effects of the diseases arising from the social evil constitute *only one of several* groups of sex problems that organized education should attempt to solve.

Concerning the other problems that sex-education should touch with great definiteness, it is my personal view that most of those outlined in the preceding lectures will be affected by instruction along five important lines, as follows:

(1) The scientific truths that lead to serious and respectful attitude on all sex questions. (2) The personal sex-hygiene that independent of social diseases conserves individual health directly or indirectly through sexual normality. (3) The ethical responsibility of individuals for the physical or social or psychical harm of their sexual actions upon other individuals, *e.g.*, in prostitution and illegitimacy. (4) The hygienic, ethical, and psychical laws that promote physical and mental health in monogamic marriage. (5) The established principles of heredity and eugenics which foretell the possible coming of a better race of humans. I believe that in these five lines there are educational problems of present and future greater significance to human health and happiness than are found in the social evil and its diseases, commandingly important though these be. Therefore, in viewing the field of sex-education with reference to the possible usefulness of knowledge in helping

Five lines of instruction.

individuals solve the vital problems that have grown naturally out of the reproductive function, I believe that we are logical only when we organize our educational aims so as to give scientific instruction concerning the problems of sex in the several lines in addition to the physical or hygienic aspects of the social evil and its diseases.

As I now see in the large the sexual problems which scientifically organized education should attack, the educational aims may be grouped under four general headings as follows:

Four aims.

First and most important, sex-education should aim to develop an open-minded, serious, scientific, and respectful attitude towards all problems of human life which relate to sex and reproduction.

Second, sex-education should aim to give that knowledge of personal hygiene of the sexual organs which is of direct value in making for the most healthful and efficient life of the individual.

Third, sex-education should aim to develop personal responsibility regarding the social, ethical, psychical, and eugenic aspects of sex as affecting the individual life in its relation to other individuals of the present and future generations; in short, sex-education should consider the problems of sexual instincts and actions in relation to society.

Fourth, sex-education should aim to teach *briefly* to young people, during later adolescence, the essential hygienic, social, and eugenic facts regarding the two destructive diseases which are chargeable to sexual promiscuity or immorality.

EDUCATIONAL ATTACK ON THE SEX PROBLEMS 95

For emphasis, let me briefly summarize these aims of sex-education: (1) Serious, scientific, and respectful attitude of mind on sex questions; (2) personal sex-hygiene; (3) social and ethical and eugenic responsibility for sex actions; (4) relation of immorality and social diseases. I have deliberately, placed these educational aims in this order because it is the order of greatest permanent importance in the sex-education movement; it represents the greatest value to the largest number of individuals who may learn the scientific truth; and it is the order most natural, most logical, and most effective in pedagogical practice with young people.

Order of importance of aims.

Sex-education organized with regard to these four aims will touch definitely all the eight problems of sex that have been discussed in preceding lectures. The first aim will directly affect the problem of vulgarity and indirectly touch those stated under the third aim. The second aim is obviously directed to the problem of personal health as it may be influenced by the sexual processes of one individual independent of others. Of course, there is also the personal aspect of social diseases, but it is clearer to consider both personal and social aspects of these diseases as a unit in the fourth aim. The third aim is based on five of the eight great problems which involve individual responsibility for the social evil, for illegitimacy, for sexual immorality, for matrimonial harmony, and for eugenics. The social

Relation of aims to problems of sex.

aspects of the venereal diseases obviously involve personal responsibility of the individual in relation to society as well as a personal hygienic problem. Thus, six of the eight great sex problems are essentially social and only those relating to personal hygiene and individual attitude are so distinctly personal as to have only an indirect relation to other individuals, as might be true in case of unharmonious marriage of individuals who are vulgar minded or who have been injured by unhygienic personal habits. Finally, the fourth aim provides for teaching the *essential* facts that may help individuals protect themselves directly, and society indirectly, against the diseases that awakened the world to the need of sex-education.

Let us turn now to analyze the aims of sex-education and consider how they may be connected with a definite scheme for sex-instruction.

§ 17. *The Aims as the Basis of Organized Sex-instruction*

I have placed first the aim to develop a serious and respectful attitude toward sex and reproduction because at the root of the sexual problems of our times is the prevailing vulgar interpretation of sex and life discussed in a preceding lecture (§ 11).

Recognizing the great importance of attitude, how may it be influenced by instruction in home or school? The most widely accepted answer is that the best beginning may be made through study of biology (including botany, zoölogy, and physiology) and through nature-study and hygiene taught on a biologic basis. No other method of introduction to sex-instruction is so natural and so likely to lead to a serious, scientific, and open-minded attitude concerning sex. *Biology and attitude.* In fact, a large part of the study of reproduction of plants and animals in courses of biology in schools and colleges has its value chiefly in the overwhelming evidence that problems of sex and reproduction are natural and dignified aspects of life. Such biological study determines attitude in no small degree. This is the chief justification for study of the reproductive processes in a series of animals and plants representing stages between the complex development of the highest animals which parallel human life and the lowest forms which the microscope reveals. In all my classes of twenty years in high school and college I have noted a marked development of serious, scientific, and open-minded attitude in response to natural and frank presentation of animal and plant life-histories. Moreover, I have many times requested large groups of students to write freely and frankly concerning the influence of biological courses upon their own attitude; and their papers have strongly supported my observation that study of animal and plant life-histories exerts a profound influence upon the attitude of students towards the human problems of sex and reproduction. If I were stating a defense for biology as one of three or four essential science courses for general education, I should place the greatest emphasis upon the study of animals and plants as a foundation for sex-instruction. Certain critics would reply that all the biological facts that are actually used in the direct human application of sex-instruction could be taught in a few lectures without a year's course in biology; but it is a demonstrated fact that a few isolated lessons do not give the attitude that comes from a good course of biology taught with the view to culminating in special sex-instruction.

Only recently has it been pointed out that one's attitude towards sex may be profoundly influenced by reading certain general literature that holds up high ideals of love and sex and life. It will be most convenient to consider the influence of literature on sex-instruction in another lecture (§ 23).

Literature and attitude.

Now let us consider the general bearings of the personal sex-hygiene demanded by the second aim. For children under ten and twelve the necessary hygiene should be presented personally (see § 25). For young people of adolescent years there are four possible ways of instruction in personal sex-hygiene: (1) It may be added naturally to a course or series of lessons in general hygiene including the problems of health for all systems of organs. (2) It may be included in a study of vertebrate and human reproduction in a course of biology or zoölogy. (3) It may be presented by a special lecture that is independent of all regular courses of study. (4) Spe-

Teaching personal sex-hygiene.

cial booklets may be put into the hands of young people. Let us now examine each of these ways:

(1) Sex-hygiene as a natural part of a series of lessons in general hygiene is most satisfactory when preceded by biological nature-study or high-school biology in which life-histories of organisms have been studied for the sake of attitude. *Sex-hygiene in general hygiene.* At present we lack satisfactory textbooks for this kind of correlation. There is a strong reaction against independent courses of hygiene in high schools, and the next plan is becoming more common.

(2) The inclusion of the necessary hygiene of all organs in courses of biology or zoölogy that have emphasized physiology and its bearings on health is the best arrangement so far *Hygiene in biology.* proposed and tested in practice. It has been tried with success by Dr. W. H. Eddy in the High School of Commerce, New York City, and by other high-school teachers working along the same lines. The arguments for teaching general hygiene on a biological basis have been presented in the last chapter of "The Teaching of Biology in Secondary Schools" by Lloyd and Bigelow, and put in textbook form in the "Applied Biology" and "Introduction to Biology" by M. A. and Anna N. Bigelow. However, personal sex-hygiene is not included in these textbooks, because educational and public opinion do not yet stand for such radical lessons in books for schools.

(3) Special lectures on sex-hygiene independent of

biology or general hygiene are at best makeshifts, and not without dangers. I fear the effect of the abrupt introduction to sex problems by special lectures, especially for girls who may be shocked much more than the average boys can be. I heartily sympathize with parents and school officials who object to special lectures that suddenly focus attention on problems of sexual health. It seems to me that special lectures should be given only when no other method of teaching is possible. This applies especially to young people who are not in schools. While I have stressed biological nature-study as offering the ideal basis for the broadest kind of sex-education, I realize that there are cases where such study cannot be held prerequisite to some aspects of sex-hygiene that young people should know. However, we should aim to make such cases the exceptions and not the rule. Some good may be accomplished by teaching certain facts of sex-hygiene frankly and directly to those who have absolutely no knowledge of nature-study and biology; but after watching the reactions of groups of boys who were receiving such information, I have been convinced that even with a limit of one hour for instruction a biological setting is decidedly important in that it gives an indirect approach.

Special lectures on hygiene.

(4) Special books and pamphlets are useful when, and only when, the above methods are impossible, but certain cautions are desirable (see § 22).

The third aim involves some difficult educational problems. Since we confess that we know so little concerning efficient methods for ethical, moral, or social teaching, it is evident that we must be far from a satisfactory plan for dealing with instruction which is intended to oppose most powerful instinctive tendencies and long-established habits of sensuality. Clearly the third aim sets no easy task for the educator; but since the possible solution of sex problems must turn on the sex actions of the individual in relation to society, the ethical-social aspects of sex-education must not be evaded because the way is not yet entirely clear. The fact is that a good beginning has been made, especially in teaching concerning social diseases, heredity, and eugenics. *Difficulty in ethical-social teaching.*

The value of all the proposed teaching concerning the relation of immorality and social diseases is more ethical than hygienic. Read any of the standard literature on the social side of venereal diseases, especially the masterly writings of the eminent physician and chief organizer of the American movement for sex-education, the late Dr. Prince A. Morrow, of New York City; and one notes that the medical facts have bearings in two directions. First, they indicate the desirability of morality as a protection of personal health; and second, they teach that the pathological results of the individual's immoral living may be passed on later to innocent wives *Social hygiene and ethics.*

and children. The first is as clearly personal hygiene as teaching that impure water may cause typhoid; but the second is social hygiene and ethics. The second is more impressive to all but the most selfish people.

There is good reason for believing that information concerning the social diseases is more likely to impress the average young man through the social-ethical appeal much more than as a matter of personal health. Therefore, a biological lesson on social diseases, which may be presented most logically in connection with other germ diseases, may have its chief value in that its meaning is social and ethical.

As another illustration of biology touching ethics, I have recently come to believe that the teaching **Biology and ethics.** concerning heredity and eugenics, which should be a standard part of the best sex-instruction, has its greatest value in the ethical appeal, and not in the direct biological application of the laws of heredity which underlie eugenics. I realize that this statement is likely to be disputed by those biologists who see in eugenics only the possibility of controlling heredity so as to propagate better strains of humans, just as breeders of plants and animals have produced better domesticated varieties. A biologist naturally believes that the ultimate aim of eugenics is improvement of physical and psychical qualities; but considering the ethical-social-biological complications of human sex-problems, it seems improbable that any decided and extensive improvement is likely to come if we continue to limit our interpretation of the principles of eugenics to the purely biological standpoint of the breeder of plants and animals. Let me illustrate by some concrete facts from eugenics:

There is a widespread opinion among science teachers that high-school biology should present some of the best established facts of heredity; and that these should be eugenically applied to human life by means of such illustrations as those afforded by the histories of certain degenerate families, such as the well-known Jukes and Kallikaks. A brief sketch of the history of the latter family, as described in Dr. Goddard's interesting book, "The Kallikak Family" (Macmillan), will make clear my point as to the ethical appeal of eugenics.

A young man of good ancestry broke the moral law about one hundred and forty years ago and became the father of an illegitimate son by a feeble-minded mother. Of 480 descendants of this son, there have been 46 normal, many immoral, many alcoholic and 143 feeble-minded. The same man who back in the revolutionary days made a moral mistake which led to such awful consequences, later married a woman of good family and became the progenitor of a second line of 496 descendants of whom 494 have been normal mentally, while two were affected by alliance with another family; and all have been first-class citizens, many of them prominent in business, professions, etc.

Eugenics and ethical teaching.

Even making due allowance for the depressing influence of the environment in which most of the down-and-out descendants in the degenerate line lived, the comparison between the normal and the abnormal lines from the same ancestor gives the most convincing eugenic evidence that has been discovered in the human race. Doubtless it will long be used as a basis for attempted biological control of the propagation of the unfit. Many similar cases of hereditary degeneracy are recorded in books on eugenics.

Such a eugenic record as that of this Kallikak family should be reviewed in every high school and college in connection with the topic "heredity" in a course of biology, for it will teach two important lessons: (1) The biological principle that defects, both physical and mental, are highly heritable, even for many generations; and (2) the ethical responsibility for the sex actions of the individual who may start a long train of human disaster that may visit the children unto even later than the third and fourth generations. The first lesson is a purely biological one which suggests the eugenic argument that defective humans, like undesirable animals and plants, should not take part in the perpetuation of the species. The second lesson is not biological but ethical, suggesting individual responsibility for conduct which may disastrously affect other individuals' lives. It seems to me that so far as general education is concerned, the ethical lesson is the more impressive and more likely to lead to voluntary eugenic practice by individuals. It is my observation that even many intelligent people are not seriously impressed by the biological evidences for eugenics considered as a general problem, but their reaction is one of interest when one begins to present the question of ethical responsibility for the transmission of physical and mental defects to future generations. Such considerations have led me to the view, already suggested, that eugenic studies in courses of biology have their greatest practical value in their ethical implications, which, of course, by influencing individual responsibility for reproduction may lead to the desirable biological improvement of the human race. Teachers of biology should present, as an economic problem, the facts which will make better breeds of plants and animals by direct application of the biological laws of heredity; but they should present and apply parallel facts to human life in order to influence first of all individual responsibility for ethical control of reproductive activity, and thus indirectly work eugenically for an improved human race.

Thus the aim of eugenics is most likely to be attained through ethical rather than biological application of the teaching which our schools can give. The men and women who view life selfishly with no feelings of ethical responsibility towards others of the present or future will take no practical interest in the biological problems of human eugenics, although the economic problems of plant and animal breeding may interest some of these same people. *Aim of eugenics.*

In addition to the ethical-social bearings of biological teaching, our sex-education will be incomplete until we learn how to attack the sex problems directly and effectively with reference to the ethical, social, psychical, and æsthetic aspects. Perhaps we may be able to do this only with mature people; probably it is too much to hope that even a serious impression will be made on all intelligent people; but somehow sex-education must be completed by adequate presentation of these aspects, for the problems of sex are satisfactorily solved only in the lives of those fortunate individuals whose vision of the relation of sex and life combines the viewpoints of biology, hygiene, psychology, ethics, religion, and last — but far from least — æsthetics.

<small>Education and other aspects of sex problems.</small>

Finally, the educational application of the fourth aim demands some explanation. Sometime in the adolescent period all young people should learn the essential facts regarding the two social diseases and their relation to immoral living. There is the widespread impression that those advocating sex-education believe in giving great prominence to the social diseases; but in opposition to this I cite the report of a committee of the American Federation for Sex Hygiene, published in the *Journal of the Society of Sanitary and Moral Prophylaxis*, January, 1913, and later reprinted as a pamphlet by the American Social Hygiene Association. In that report there are *twenty-three* recommendations concerning sex-

<small>Only essential knowledge of social diseases.</small>

instruction; but *only* one mentions social diseases and in these words: "During the later period of adolescence . . . there should be given . . . special instruction as to the character and dangers of the venereal diseases." That seems sufficient. It is not desirable that young people should review the horrible facts relating to perverted sexuality. Ten or twenty brief and authoritative statements quoted impressively from medical and social literature ought to give fair warning of lurking dangers in immoral living. More extensive information has often proved dangerous. I would gladly advocate that this dark side of life be kept in sealed books if I did not know that so many young people need forewarning and definite guidance. Our educational system will not do its full duty if it fails to offer the needed help so that it may be obtained by all adolescent young people who are not so fortunate as to be guided by parents and other personal teachers.

IV

THE TEACHER OF SEX-KNOWLEDGE

§ 18. *Who Should Give Sex-instruction?*

A large number of people have been convinced that young people need knowledge which will help them face the great problems of sex; but they withhold their approval of the sex-education movement because they are not satisfied that proper teachers exist. It is, therefore, evident that we cannot make permanent progress by emphasizing the need of sex-education unless we can give assurance that qualified teachers are available.

The situation as regards teachers of sex-instruction is very different from that of all other subjects concerning which young people should be taught. We cannot safely plan the teaching regarding sex until we know the teacher. This will be evident, I think, after some general considerations concerning selection of teachers and some discussion of problems such as the first teacher, teachers for classes, and some undesirable teachers. The general rule should be, first, find the safe and sure teacher and, second, select the facts and plan the lessons that the chosen teacher may give effectively.

The teacher most important.

So far as young children are concerned, the needed instruction is so general in character that the sex of the competent teacher is of little im- Teachers of portance, but the information that ought same sex for to prepare for and guide through the children. mazes of adolescent youth should come to young people from teachers of the same sex. If exceptions must be made rather than omit instruction altogether, some very mature women may safely guide both boys and girls through adolescence; but men, even physicians, should not undertake instruction of adolescent young women, unless parents and other mature people are present to help with attitude. That women may well instruct boys I know, because the most impressive sex lecture I ever heard was given by the late Dr. Mary Wood-Allen to the boys of the freshman class when I was a college student. But note that I have said "some very mature women." The fact is that I fear danger for some boys if they are frankly instructed by attractive young women who are only ten to fifteen years older than their pupils. Hence, I urge great caution if there must be any exceptions to the general rule that teachers and pupils should be of the same sex.

I realize the difficulty of applying this rule in many high schools where the foundations of sex-education are well laid on the biological Coeducabasis. There is no reason why the bio- tional logical studies should not be coeduca- classes. tional through nature-study and biology as far as the development of frogs and birds and, in a general way, of mammals. In fact, both of my textbooks, the "Applied Biology" and the "Introduction to Biology," which emphasize reproduction of organisms more than other high-school books, have been used throughout in coeducational classes. However, these books stop where the problems of human life begin and should be supplemented by lessons for sex-limited classes. There are writers who suggest that segregation of the sexes for teaching concerning human life may be at present a necessity because complete frankness on sexual questions is certainly obstructed by tradition; but we must not ignore the deep social reasons why, in general, there must be maintained a certain amount of reserve between the sexes in the consideration of some important problems of life. No educational theory or practice can possibly alter the fundamental physical or psychical relations of the sexes which nature seems to have fixed immutably.

One other point that deserves attention in this connection is the common statement that only **Married women as teachers.** married women, preferably mothers, can be competent instructors of young women. This strikes me as more than absurd. Personal experience is not always necessary for teaching in any line. The greatest medical teachers have not had the diseases they describe so clearly. The best elementary teachers and specialists on the care of children are not always mothers; on the contrary, some of these are men.

The fact is that these teachers have learned, not from personal experience, but from the great accumulations of scientific knowledge of medicine, hygiene, and education. There is an abundance of such knowledge relating to sex that may be clearly understood by bright women who have no bi-personal knowledge of sex. Therefore, I believe that it is nonsense to insist that only women with complete sexual experiences can be efficient guides for other women.

§ 19. *The Child's First Teachers of Sex-knowledge*

The first instruction which may begin to lay the foundation for the individual's sex-education should be given in early childhood by parents, or by other adults, who happen to be on the most intimate personal terms with the child. Usually this means the mother; {Mothers and other first teachers.} but there are numerous cases of teachers, governesses, grandmothers, and even fathers who have greater personal influence with certain children than their mothers have. The essential point is that the child should be instructed only by an adult who can exert the greatest personal influence.

Many parents who believe in sex-education for their children hold that the mothers should give all necessary hygienic guidance and teach the elementary facts of life to the children of both sexes in the pre-adolescent years, {Mothers and adolescent boys.} but that with the dawn of adolescence the girls should continue to be instructed by their mothers, while the boys should be guided by their fathers. So far as girls are concerned, this seems to be a fairly good plan; but nine times out of ten it is not best for the boys for several reasons: First, the sudden change of attitude on the part of the mother will surely impress upon the boy that there is something about sex in boys that even his mother dares not talk over with him. At about this same time when the mother begins to avoid the sex question with her boy, he will surely begin to get vulgar information and impressions from his boy companions. He will in all probability begin to hear the impure and obscene stories and vulgar language that are so common among many men and boys, and he will be sure to learn that the vulgarity which he hears must not be repeated in the presence of his mother and sisters. It is a most critical time in the mental attitude of the boy. His mother has so far been directing him towards purity and then suddenly sets him adrift. If there is ever a time in a boy's life when he needs intimacy with his mother, it is in the early adolescent years of twelve to fourteen. A strong mother's heart to heart guidance at that time will influence the boy more than all the sex-education which the schools and colleges combined can ever hope to offer. Such is the problem of home teaching for adolescent boys. I emphatically protest against the foolish and even dangerous idea that because a boy is beginning to metamorphose into a man his mother should cease to help him with the problems of sex. Lucky is that adolescent boy whose mother realizes her duty and her opportunity and holds him as intimately as if he were a girl of corresponding age.

§ 20. *Selecting Teachers for Class Instruction*

The references to "the teacher" in the following are primarily applicable to those who may be called upon to give sex-instruction as class work in schools, colleges, churches, the Y.M.C.A., the Y.W.C.A., and other educational organizations.

The chief question for discussion in this lecture is that of selecting the teacher of those phases of sex-instruction that are directly related to human life, that is, personal sex-hygiene and sex-ethics. So far as biological facts of sex are concerned, there are no special problems such as may not be handled by teachers of biology in general according to the accepted methods (see Lloyd and Bigelow, "Teaching of Biology in the Secondary School" and Bigelow, "Teacher's Manual of Biology").

As already suggested, a large part of the sex-instruction is simply an extension of biological science, hygiene, and ethics; and in secondary schools and colleges should be given by selected teachers of the regular staff and whenever possible as a part of regular courses. *Regular teachers if possible.* There may be some necessary modifications to this plan; for example, in Teachers College the course on sex-education and another series of lectures on sex-physiology and hygiene for women are open to students who do not take the biology courses in which the sex-instruction logically belongs.

The culminating stages of any complete scheme for formal sex-education of young people will be sex-hygiene considered in its strict sense as that special phase of sex-education which deals with problems of health, and sex-ethics which determines the responsibility of individuals for control of sexual instincts. While nature-study and biology and general hygiene may be organized so as to present the major portion of the facts which should be included in a complete scheme of sex-instruction in schools and colleges, the application of these facts to personal life is the most difficult problem of sex-education. In fact, it is the only real problem, for long before sex-education became a definite movement the most efficient science teachers were presenting the fundamental facts on which we now propose to build with certain hygienic and ethic instruction which directly touches the personal life of the student. As already said, the human application will require only a few lessons, preferably in connection with nature-study, biology, ethics, or hygiene. But although brief, such instruction is the keystone in the arch of sex-education, and it is very important that there be no serious mistakes in selecting the teachers.

Sex specialists not desirable.

I have mentioned special teachers as necessary for instruction with direct reference to human life. I hasten to add that I still agree with the report of the special committee (Morrow, *et al.*) of the American Federation for Sex Hygiene that it is not desirable that any teacher should make a specialty of this type of instruction and of no other. We do not want "sex specialists" in the schools (see pp. 10 and 20–23 of the Report of the Committee). It is important that all teachers should have general information regarding the sex problems of young people in order to be able to help individual pupils.

§ 21. *Certain Undesirable Teachers for Special Hygienic and Ethical Instruction*

It will be most helpful if we consider the problem of selecting teachers with a view to rejecting those who certainly should not undertake the special hygienic and ethical teaching, for teachers who are good in other subjects and who are fortunately free from certain disqualifications discussed in the following, may by means of study adapt themselves for the final and most important stages of sex-education.

There are five types of teachers who should be regarded as disqualified for teaching personal sex-hygiene and sex-ethics.

First, those men and women who are unable to speak of sex-hygiene as calmly and seriously as they do of any other phase of hygiene had better not undertake the instruction of young people. There are many such men and women among teachers who, so far as scientific training is concerned, ought to be good teachers of sex-hygiene. As an illustration of this attitude that leaves the wrong impression

Embarrassed teachers.

with students, it is reported that a good teacher of hygiene recently prefaced a brief talk to college girls as follows: "I shall now consider a process that no cultured woman ever mentions except with bated breath. I refer to menstruation."

The second kind of people who should not teach sex-hygiene are the men and women who are the unfortunate victims of sexual abnormality, either physical or psychical, that more or less influences their outlook on life. Certain neurotic and hysterical men or women who lack thorough physiological training and whose own sexual disturbances have **Abnormal teachers.** led them to devour omnivorously and unscientifically the psychopathological literature of sex by such authors as Havelock Ellis, Krafft-Ebing, and Freud, are probably unsafe teachers of sex-hygiene. Especially is this true of the women of this type whose introspective morbidity has led them to diagnose their own functional disturbances as the direct result of "oversexuality" and restraint from normal sexual expression — a diagnosis that is probably wrong nine times in ten cases. Such a woman is a very dangerous teacher of sex-hygiene for adolescent girls; and a positive menace to older unmarried women who, if free from absorbing work, may spend their leisure in becoming more or less restless under the unsocial, if not unphysiologic, conditions of unwelcome celibacy. This is no imaginary danger. The reader of this will not be interested in details, but the author has received from physicians and others reliable information concerning several extremely abnormal women of the above-described type who are taking an active interest in the sex-instruction of young people and are actually suggesting to their friends among young women the dangerous and untrue doctrine that prolonged celibacy for women results in repressed sexuality that surely leads to ill health. Such ideas, it is true, are traceable to certain well-known radical writers on the psychopathology of sex; but we must remember that the great majority of physicians and other scientific investigators who have studied such problems refuse to believe that repressed sex instincts in either men or women do the harm that a few extremists have claimed. But even if it were known beyond the shadow of a doubt that repressed sex instincts may injure people, it would be unwise to intrust young people to instruction by teachers who have a hypochondriacal interest in such a doctrine of repression. Such suggestions can do only harm to the vast majority of persons who receive them. To say the least, it is unfortunate that the psychopathology of sex has become so widely circulated among those who are not well trained in physiology and psychiatry.

The third kind of people who should not be intrusted with teaching sex-hygiene are the men and women who, without a scientific perspective, have plunged into the literature of sexual abnormality until they have come to think that knowledge concerning perverted life is an important part of sex-education for young people, especially for those of post-adolescent years. I know of teachers and physicians who advise young people not much over twenty years of age to read such psychopathological works as those of Krafft-Ebing, Ellis, and Freud, and various works dealing with commercialized vice. Here is a grave danger. The less that people without professional use for knowledge of sexual pathology know concerning it, the better it will be for their peace of mind and possibly for their morals. Therefore, I urge that he who enthusiastically studies the abnormalities of sex life without reference to scientific research or professional demands, is not likely to be the kind of teacher who will present abnormal life only so far as is necessary to an understanding of the perfectly normal.

Teachers who emphasize sexual abnormality.

The fourth kind of people who ought not to instruct the young in personal problems of sex-hygiene are the men and women whose own unhappy romances or married life, or whose knowledge of vice conditions, have made them pessimistic concerning sex-problems. There are in our schools and colleges to-day some such men and many such women, and there will be danger for young people when the growing freedom of expression allows these sexual pessimists to impress their own hopeless philosophy of sex upon students. The educational world does not need such teachers, but rather those who can follow the late Dr. Morrow

Pessimistic teachers.

THE TEACHER OF SEX-KNOWLEDGE 119

in seeing a bright side of life that almost dispels the darkness of sexual errors.

The fifth kind of persons who ought not to teach the personal side of sex-hygiene are those who cannot command the most serious respect of their pupils. This applies especially to many men teachers whose flippant attitude and even questionable living are not likely to help their pupils, especially boys, towards a satisfactory interpretation of sex problems. Of course, such teachers ought not be in schools at all, but the fact is that for various reasons they sometimes get there and stay there; and so they must be weighed by the school official who selects the teachers to be intrusted with special problems of sex-education. *Teachers not respected by pupils.*

Summarizing, I have in this lecture aimed to warn the school administrator, and others who must select teachers of classes, against the kinds of teachers who ought not be chosen for presenting the special problems of sex-education, especially those of sex-hygiene and sex-ethics. I have pointed out that there are five serious disqualifications; and it is probable that if strictly applied when choosing teachers for special sex-instruction, there will be elimination of three or four in every ten of those whose training in science might be expected to qualify them as teachers of this special line. It is a fair question as to what a school or other institution should do if it has no teachers who are free from the above *No instruction without satisfactory teachers.*

disqualifications. My own belief is that it is better to get an outsider for the handling of the special problems. If this is impracticable, then suggest to the students that they read certain books such as are recommended in the last sections of this book. Even entire omission of the study of the personal and social aspects of sex-hygiene and sex-ethics is far wiser than intrusting a class to a teacher with one or more of the negative qualifications that we have been considering in this lecture. The effect of sex-education upon individual lives will in no small degree depend upon the impression made by the living teacher who deals with the difficult problems of sex in relation to hygiene and ethics. Hence, the greatest care should be taken when selecting the teacher for this all-important part of the student's sex-education.

V

BOOKS AS TEACHERS CONCERNING SEX AND LIFE

§ 22. *Value and Danger of Special Sex Books for Young People*

There are many parents and teachers who believe that young people should get their sexual information by private reading, and numerous books for boys and girls have been prepared to meet such a demand. The desire for such "private" reading undoubtedly exists, especially in boys; but this is part of the general air of secrecy and vulgarity that has enshrouded the truth about sexual matters. Many eminent physicians agree that there are elements of physical and perhaps moral danger when a boy reads a sex-science book secretly, but that there are few such possibilities in frank and scientific teaching by a competent instructor. This is recognized by leaders in the Y.M.C.A., and they prefer to read books with the boys in study classes. Many scientific women think there is no such danger for average girls, but agree that girls as well as boys will gain in respect for the subject of sex if the atmosphere of secrecy can be avoided. Hence,

<small>Books for private reading.</small>

while books for private reading are better than ignorance, they alone will not solve many of the problems at which sex-education is directed. We must cease to foster the secrecy created by an atmosphere of obscenity, and the study of sex must be brought into the light of day. Let good books be recommended through parents and with their approval be issued freely by libraries and without restrictions which suggest something dark and wrong. Let parents and teachers encourage such reading, but not as something requiring secrecy. Rather let such books be read as freely as any other good books, and let parents and competent teachers follow the young readers closely so as to explain facts and help develop the desirable attitude of mind. Especially let parents encourage the idea that approved sex-science books may be read at the family fireside as properly as any other books. Above all, let parents and teachers work in every possible way against the time-worn idea that problems of sex are essentially vulgar and demand secrecy even in scientific study. We must have a nobler and healthier outlook on human life than that which so commonly prevails, and we can never get it by secret study of sex-science by young people. Such study may do some good by warning against unhygienic habits and social diseases; but it is certainly inadequate to give the open-minded attitude needed so much for appreciating the ethical, social, and æsthetic bearings of human life as it is influenced by normal sexual functions.

It has been urged by well-known teachers that, for sex-instruction, pamphlets are better than books in that they do not hold the attention too long on topics that may be exciting to some young people. *Pamphlets vs. books.* On the other hand, books usually make a stronger appeal, while pamphlets are likely to be regarded lightly, as are magazines and newspapers. There is no doubt that most sex books for young people are too extended, and there is need of condensed forty-and fifty-cent booklets in place of the books commonly sold at one dollar. Three or four small booklets by different authors read at widely separated intervals will interest and influence a young man more than one large and comprehensive book. There is besides great value in the points of view of various authors.

At present there are no thoroughly satisfactory books for adolescent boys and girls. In my opinion, W. S. Hall's books for boys are the most reliable, and his "Life Problems" is the best selection of facts for girls; but some mature readers criticize the style of presentation. Some other books for adolescent young people are mentioned with critical notes in the *Better books needed.* bibliography at the end of this book. There is still plenty of chance for authors to experiment in writing books of this class.

§ 23. *General Literature and Sex Problems*

In the world's best literature there is much that teaches important lessons in the field of the larger **Sex in** sex-education. In the guise of love, sex **literature.** problems have always held the prominent place in all literature. Many a great book teaches direct or positive lessons by holding up high ideals for inspiration and imitation; but some of the most impressive lessons are in negative form, especially in fiction that deals with the tragedies of life.

As examples of literature of direct influence in helping many young people solve the problems of **Religious** sex, we think first of that which holds up **books.** high ideals of personal purity, such as the Bible and other religious books. There is no doubt that such literature has a tremendous influence on many young people; but it has little influence on others, probably in part because the somewhat mystical style of most religious writings is meaningless to many people.

It is a fact that many young people who refuse to be interested in religious literature may be influ- **Appeal of** enced for sexual purity by the emotional **poetry.** appeal of some general literature. This is especially true of romantic poetry. I believe that the high "idealism" of love inspired by Tennyson's "The Princess" and "Idylls of the King," by Longfellow's "Evangeline" and "The Hanging of the Crane," by some of Shakespeare's plays, and by other great poetry with similar themes has had and will continue to have greater influence on the attitude and ethics of many young people than all the formal sex-teaching that can be organized. Hence, I believe that teachers of literature should be led to take interest in the larger sex-education to the end that by selection and interpretation of great masterpieces they may contribute in a valuable way to the solution of some of the problems that have their center in the deeper nature of sex.

Interpretation of literature by teachers is very important for the purposes of sex-education of young people. As an example, take Tennyson's "Idylls of the King," whose movement centers in the life problems that turn around love. *Importance of interpretation.* The average reader is likely to miss the great lessons if the poem is not critically interpreted either by living teachers or by such critical essays as those by Henry van Dyke in his "Poetry of Tennyson" and Newell Dwight Hillis in his "Great Books as Life-Teachers." Without interpretation "The Idylls" may teach false as well as true lessons of life. Some of the Knights of the Round Table (Galahad and Percivale) were worthy followers of the good and pure King Arthur, and some of them (like Lancelot and Tristram and Merlin) proved unable to live up to the vow of chastity to which Arthur swore all his knights. And on the part of the ladies of Arthur's court, there was purity and devotion and true womanhood in Elaine and Enid, while Guinevere and Ettarre and Vivien were unchaste and faithless.

In fact, all phases of the relations of men and women in the struggles and perplexities of life are pictured; and therefore it is important that a well-trained teacher should be the guide and interpreter if the "Idylls of the King" are to be read with the idea of understanding their true bearings on life, which includes their contribution to the larger sex-education.

I have used "The Idylls of the King" as an illustration because they are so many-sided in sex problems; but much other great literature may be made to help young people to high ideals of relationships between men and women. I have emphasized the place of such literature in the larger sex-education because I have come to believe that interpretation of life either real or in great literature may have profound influence in the development of one's philosophy of life. As a matter of educational procedure insuring that young people will learn to interpret life, especially those aspects that the larger sex-education touches so definitely, there appears to be no more natural and unobtrusive way of approach than that offered by the study of literature. I am convinced that many teachers of literature may be efficient workers in the cause of the larger sex-education, supplementing the scientific teaching in the ethical lines where science is admittedly weak, if not helpless. It is to be hoped that numerous teachers will soon grasp this opportunity. If they will study the sex-education movement in order to get its general bearings and will teach the sex aspect of literature on a basis of high ideals of life and love, we need have no fear as to the culmination of the instruction which properly begins with study of the biological facts of life in its sexual aspects and leads on and on to its climax in the ethical aspects of the individual's sex life in relation to other individuals, that is, to society.

I take it for granted that no teacher of literature who contributes to sex-instruction will let the students know that the emphasis placed on great life problems is part of a conspiracy of parents and educators to give in the name of sex-education instruction that will help prepare the individual for facing the problems. *Not to be labeled "sex-education."* Here, as elsewhere, the young people had better be left unaware that their elders are so interested in giving them instruction regarding sex problems that they have organized, for study of ways and means, a movement known as sex-education.

The abundant literature that points to the moral to be drawn from sexual tragedies has doubtless influenced thousands of young people. I have talked with many educated people who confessed to having been profoundly influenced by such books as Eliot's "Adam Bede," Hawthorne's "Scarlet Letter," Goethe's "Faust," Hardy's "Tess of the d'Urbervilles." One might go on and compile an extensive bibliography, for fiction of all languages *Sex tragedies of fiction* of all times is full of the errors into which insistent sex instincts have drawn men and women who were not masters of themselves. All standard fiction in which sexual errors and their penalties are associated may do good as a part of the larger sex-education, but the teacher should make sure that the young readers arrive at the correct interpretation.

Against that type of fiction which presents sex problems that do not clearly "point a moral," the average so-called "problem novel" of recent time, there should be general opposition by workers for the larger sex-education. Many of the modern novels and magazine stories seem to introduce sexual situations for the same reason that Boccaccio did in some of his tales, namely, the attractiveness of lasciviousness. Unlike the commendable novels, it is characteristic of the equivocal ones that no penalty is demanded or paid and no moral conclusion is suggested. In fact, the way is very often left open to an immoral interpretation. All such literature certainly tends to work against the aims of sex-education. Perhaps parents and teachers may coöperate to keep much of this kind of literature out of the hands of young people, but the safest procedure is in cultivating taste for literature that does teach helpful lessons of life. If young people do read books and magazines that seem to stand for uncertain morals, it is best that parents and teachers should point out the moral interpretations.

Fiction without a moral.

§ 24. *Dangers in Literature on Abnormal Sexuality*

The opinion is spreading among those who are studying the educational problems relating to sex that there is great danger, even for many adults, in much of the literature describing psychopathological and abnormal social-sexual facts. There are enormous quantities of such literature, particularly concerning the social evil. It is extremely doubtful whether the reader who is not directly engaged in medicine, psychiatry, or social reform will profit by filling his mind with facts from the darkest side of life. No doubt it is important that all intelligent men and women should know enough about sexual immorality and the life of the underworld so that they will realize the necessity of protecting young people from vice in all its forms; but this does not mean that everybody should read extensively in the mass of printed matter that sets forth the most awful details concerning human depravity. There is a real danger in this line. The sex-education movement has already brought the problems of sex out of the old-time secrecy, and no other topics of the times are so freely read and discussed. This might be well if the reading and discussion always took constructive lines leading towards improvement of sexual relationships; but unfortunately, much of the present popular interest in sexual problems seems to be a morbid craving for the abnormal. We find this tendency in the demand for

Danger in present interests in the abnormal.

K

a certain type of sex-problem novels, we see it frequently on the stage and in motion pictures, and we hear it in general conversation. The advertised suggestion of sexual immorality in a forthcoming serial novel often raises surprisingly the circulation of certain magazines. A few hints of sexual irregularity in certain plays have brought crowded audiences. A scandalous divorce case, reported as freely as the law allows, is a choice morsel for average readers of newspapers. Everywhere it is the sexual abnormality, perversity, and even bestial vulgarity, that seems to attract the most attention. Books and magazines and theaters and preachers who extol the normal and bright side of sex-life are not now extremely popular with the masses of people. As a well-known magazine recently summarized the present situation, "it has struck sex o'clock in America." There is no denying the fact that in recent years the popular interest in sex problems has taken a dangerous turn. It is time for those who are active in the sex-education movement to note the signs of the times, for an effective educational scheme for young people must take into account the present tendency towards a dangerous interest in literature relating to sexual abnormality, especially immorality. All this tendency towards interest in the abnormal or irregular sexual problems must cause not a little worry to those whose interest is primarily in securing widespread recognition of the advantages of normal and moral living.

Perhaps those who are seriously interested in sex-education may help stem the tide towards interest in sexual abnormality by using greater care in the selection of literature, both for young people and for their elders. I recently met a superintendent of schools who had carefully read certain large volumes on the medical, psychical, and social abnormalities of sex, and many books and pamphlets on the social evil. Altogether he had read more than five thousand pages on the immoral and abnormal aspects of sex. He wanted to know where he might find a book on the normal side of sex in its physiological, psychological, and ethical aspects. Unfortunately, there is no such treatise by an author whose scientific standing equals that of several of those who have written extensively on the abnormal side; and probably this is in part the reason why so many young men and women are now molding their ideas of sexual life according to the patterns described by the authors of works on social and sexual pathology. Not a month passes in which I am not astounded to find men and women who have plunged deeply into studies of sexual vice and pathology and who know less of the normal biology of sex than is contained in such books as W. S. Hall's "Sexual Knowledge" or the last chapter of Martin's "Human Body, Advanced Course." This is indeed a strange situation, and we might compare it with reading extensive works on insanity before learning the elements of normal

Need of interest in normal sex life.

psychology. It is certainly a useless, if not a dangerous line of approach to the information. concerning sex which intelligent people need. The leaders in the sex-education movement will do well to promote the circulation of some brief and authoritative statement of the chief facts relating to the problems of abnormal sexual life and then to discourage the popular circulation of the extensive works which only certain physicians and social reformers need. I know that there is some difference of opinion as to the effect of such literature. I know many prominent educators and physicians who would keep the extensive works on the psychopathology of sex out of the hands of all general readers; but I also know a few who see no possibility of danger in widespread circulation of such books.

Looking at all sides of the present situation, it is my personal conclusion that every one should learn first the scientific facts regarding normal processes connected with the sexual system; and then for the general reader there should be only a limited amount of warning knowledge regarding the dangers of sexual abnormalities.

Limited knowledge of the abnormal.

VI

Sex–Instruction for Pre–Adolescent Years

In § 8 of the Report of the Committee of Three of the American Federation for Sex-hygiene, by Morrow and others, the life of the child was divided into four periods, namely, — under six years, from six to twelve, twelve to sixteen, sixteen to maturity. *Periods of early life.* This division now seems to me to be too arbitrary, and I have come to believe that it is more helpful to consider sex-instruction for three periods as follows: pre-adolescence (ending at eleven to fourteen years); early adolescence (twelve to sixteen years for girls, thirteen to seventeen for boys); later adolescence (sixteen to twenty-one for girls, eighteen to twenty-five for boys).

§ 25. *Elementary Instruction and Influence*

The life-histories of plants and animals as taught in the best nature-study [1] are important in forming attitude towards reproduction and giving a basis for simple and truthful answers to the child's questions as to the origin of the indi- *Nature-study.*

[1] See books on nature-study, *e.g.*, Holtz's "Nature-Study," Hodge's "Nature-Study and Life," Comstock's "Handbook of Nature-Study." Morley's "Renewal of Life," March's "Towards Racial Health," and Hall's "The Doctor's Daughter" suggest the main lines of the nature-study approach to sex-education.

vidual human life. The publications listed in the last section of this book under the headings "For Girls" and "For Boys" will help parents and teachers.

There is need of little private hygienic instruction, but of much guidance away from harmful habits. This will be indicated in the next section which considers masturbation as it concerns children of both sexes and all ages.

The protection of children from corrupting influences is an important work of sex-education in preadolescent years. Probably the greatest safety lies in parents giving simple facts regarding reproduction and in cultivating confidence so that any accidental contact of their children with vulgarity will be counteracted in advance. Many parents, especially mothers, have found this possible.

Protection.

In the years between ten and twelve every child should learn from a parent or other adult confidant some general facts regarding their approaching puberty. This is especially important in the case of girls, for many a girl has been physically and mentally injured because a prudish mother has procrastinated too long the giving of information regarding the first menstrual period. The facts in the first thirty pages of W. S. Hall's "Life Problems" should be known by many girls of eleven and by the great majority before thirteen. Some books for young girls are defective in that they avoid reference to

Girls' preparation for puberty.

the coming changes. I see no excuse for a sex-hygiene book for girls who are too young to be trusted with the simplest knowledge regarding menstruation. Such children should be interested in nature studies and perhaps the elements of general hygiene, but certainly not in books with curiosity-stimulating titles.

Since boys entering puberty pass through no such sharply defined beginning as girls do, the information they need in advance is not so specific. At the same time, we must recognize that the average boy under twelve years picks up more information regarding sexual life than a girl does, and so the problem of teaching self-control comes earlier, although the average girl enters puberty a year or two before the boy. Parents and teachers must recognize the fact that sexual tendencies come to many boys several years before puberty, and masturbation and even premature sexual intercourse are possible problems with many boys long before the twelfth year. The boy's early gathering of sexual information is not without advantage, for it becomes possible for parents and other adult confidants to explain many important truths as to the proper use of his sex organs and as to his conduct towards girls. All this can be done with the average boy of eleven or twelve and with hundreds of even nine and ten without any fear of giving information that is startlingly new and without any danger of giving a nervous shock.

Special needs of boys.

It is not so with average girls of equal ages, if we may accept the opinion of many women who are trained in science and medicine. Specific information as to the functional relationships of the two sexes is said by many educated women to have been absolutely new and startling to them at twenty and twenty-five years. Evidently there is a special reason for gradual and cautious teaching of girls, and so it is probably best, as many parents urge, that in pre-adolescent years the girl's instruction in social-sexual lines be training in modest deportment and a proper reserve towards boys. This ought to be sufficient for the girl's protection until gradually in adolescent years she learns the whole story of life, probably several years later than her boy friends whose natural leadership in sexual activity makes their early information desirable as a protection to both sexes.

Cautious teaching of girls.

In the pre-adolescent years parents and teachers should coöperate in developing a spirit of group fellowship between boys and girls and at the same time instill into the boys something of that chivalrous and protective attitude of boys towards girls such as one finds in the families of the highest culture. I emphatically mean "group fellowship," for it is certainly undesirable to encourage in pre-adolescents any tendency towards paired comradeship. It is certainly best that boys and girls should have many good friends of both sexes. The real truth back of the old adage "two is company and three is a crowd"

Children's friendships.

makes the "crowd" highly desirable for both pre-adolescence and early adolescence, for in these years it is friendship and not romantic love that will be most helpful in the later life. As one step in this direction, all sensible adults should show their disfavor to the abominable habit of teasing small children concerning their best friends of the other sex. Parents and teachers will do some of the best work in the larger sex-education if they begin in pre-adolescent years to develop the social life of the children along lines similar to those suggested above.

Summarizing, it is evident that there is very little direct sex-instruction suitable for pre-adolescent years. So far as the child's own life is concerned, it now seems clear that parents or other adult confidants must instruct individuals, or possibly small uniformly selected groups. Class instruction seems out of the question except for life-history studies of animals and plants. On the whole, then, there is nothing radical or impossible in the proposition that there should be a beginning of sex-education before the advent of adolescence. *Summary.*

§ 26. *Hygienic and Educational Treatment of Unhealthful Habits*

All adults should take a sane and scientific view of the sex problems that are likely to come even to normal children. We must remember that they are born with sexual mechanisms that may easily and automatically lead into harmful habits unless parents and teachers guide *Problems of children.*

hygienically and mentally along the lines that are known to offer safety.

Concerning habitual manipulation of the sexual organs of either sex, known in medical literature as masturbation or self-abuse (often erroneously called "onanism"), there are certain facts that are important for the guidance of all parents and teachers. I discuss it in this connection since the problem often arises in the later years of the pre-adolescent period.

Masturbation.

It is absurd to suppose that the tendency towards the habit means degeneracy or innate viciousness of children. Young horses, dogs, monkeys, and other animals sometimes form a similar habit, the stimulus being some irritation of the sexual organs. Hence, it is not at all unnatural when children attempt to relieve their irritated organs by friction, and then it is inevitable that the sensitive nerve endings will give sensations that are more or less pleasurable and satisfying, depending upon the sex, age, and emotional peculiarity of the individual child. This fact suggests to parents and teachers the methods of prophylaxis; namely, avoid (1) irritation of sexual organs and (2) opportunity for manipulation.

Does not indicate degeneracy.

With regard to irritation, the first sign of such disturbance may appear in babyhood. In the case of boys, whose structure renders them vastly more liable than girls to external irritation, the family physician should make sure during infancy whether circumcision

Irritation.

or a stretching of the prepuce (foreskin) may be desirable. According to Dr. Emmet Holt, the eminent pediatrician, about one male baby in four or five is born with an elongated or tight prepuce that needs surgical attention. A corresponding abnormality of the clitoris is sometimes found in baby girls. Some radical surgeons advocate universal circumcision of boys because they believe that it reduces local irritation, favors cleanliness, tends to prevent masturbation, and reduces susceptibility to the venereal diseases. There is certainly some truth in these claims; but some conservative surgeons point out that for the great majority of boys all these advantages may be obtained by reasonable attention to hygienic habits, that orthodox Jewish and other circumcised boys are by no means free from harmful habits, that some boys are more irritable after circumcision, that preputial stretching is often a good substitute for circumcision, and that the taunts of other boys often make circumcised boys too conscious of their own mutilation. A scientific doctor who has no special financial interest in the increase of surgical operations and who carefully reviews both the radical and conservative literature relating to circumcision, will not hasten to submit boys to this operation until it is certain that their sexual organs happen to have congenital deformity that only radical surgical treatment can correct.

Circumcision.

In addition to making sure that uncleanliness or structural abnormality are not responsible for irritation of sex organs, there are some special hygienic rules useful for parents and teachers who have charge **Hygienic rules.** of children. Most important is avoidance of habit formation. Clothing should be well adjusted to avoid pressure and friction of the sexual organs, and so constructed (especially night clothing) that it is not convenient for the hands to reach the organs. Normal boys require pockets, but they should open at the waistband and not at the side of the hips. The reason for these suggestions is evident. When we recall that little children naturally tend to explore themselves, such as by putting fingers into the mouth, feeling their toes, inserting foreign objects into nose and ears, and when we also recall how quickly a child may learn the habit of sucking its thumb, we must realize the importance of guarding the child from extending such activities to its sexual organs, which, because they possess the most sensitive nerve endings in the body, are most liable to lead to habitual manipulation. In the light of such facts, it is nonsense to assume, as so many good mothers have done, that only innately vicious children learn masturbation. The truth is that in the case of most children under twelve this habit has an origin no more vicious than such habits as thumb-sucking; and in all cases of habits, parents **Other suggestions for parents.** and others responsible for the children should be given the blame.

The following suggestions in addition to those above are likely to help parents do much towards avoiding or solving the early sex problems of their children. These facts apply also to later years.

Have children sleep on a hard mattress. The old-time feather bed was dangerous. There should be light-weight covers, and the room cool. Children should sleep on either side, *rarely* in the unnatural back position. Aim to have regular sleeping hours; but do not send children to bed unsupervised when they are excited and not tired enough for immediate sleep. Have them arise as soon as wide awake in the morning. Never punish children by sending them to bed.

Do not leave children to their own devices; they may naturally fall into dangerous play. Privacy is often demanded by the moods of adults, but it is dangerous for children. **Dangers of privacy.** A certain camp for boys has the commendable rule that the boys have no privacy during the entire summer. Many educators and physicians condemn private bedrooms or cubicles in schools for boys.

A strenuous life of physical and mental activity is the best solution of personal control of sexual instincts. Reasonable athletics and study make an ideal combination for **Athletics.** both boys and girls. And yet we must not trust absolutely to athletics or other physical work, for there are certainly many individuals whose sexual desires are not controlled by muscular exercise. Much of the formal athletic training may have no more influence on sexual control than dogmatic creeds.

Strong condiments and alcoholic drinks are known to be sexual excitants for many people, and for this and other hygienic reasons should be forbidden to children. There is a widespread, but still undemonstrated opinion that tea, coffee, tobacco, and strong condiments have an exciting effect. However, there is plenty of scientific authority, based on other hygienic grounds, for avoiding these at least during the years of growth.

Drugs.

Constipation is likely to cause sexual irritation, and hence this is an additional reason for submitting children to competent doctors for treatment of this disturbance which so seriously affects general health, especially by auto-intoxication.

Constipation.

Cool bathing in the morning, especially of the sexual organs, is hygienic, except for girls during the monthly periods (including two days before the expected menstrual onset). For various reasons, bathing in very warm water should be very limited, and then only for cleansing.

Bathing.

In hygienic instructions to children, avoid giving them any ideas concerning the supposed prevalence of the habit of masturbation. There is a dangerous tendency to follow the crowd.

Form of instruction.

Also, the habit should never be described to children except as "unnecessary handling of the sex organs." It is dangerous to suggest to children, as certain books do, that there is any pleasurable sensation resulting from manual manipulation of the organs, for the force of suggestion or curiosity has led some children to experiment with themselves until they formed the habit.

There are no absolutely certain signs or symptoms, and those suggested by certain authors, especially by quack doctors, make young people and even parents and teachers judge some individuals in an unfortunate way. Especially should parents and teachers remember that there is absolutely no scientific basis for supposing that great diffidence, indigestion, pimples on the face, boys' lack of interest in girls, and numerous other popular "signs," are indications of the masturbation habit. Like the symptoms in patent-medicine advertising, the above "signs" are so general that they are sure to fit some cases. *Symptoms.*

Do not tell children the ancient falsehood that insanity will surely result from handling the sexual organs. It is true that masturbation is a common habit of certain types of insane people and of some neurotics; but it is probable that the habit is more often one of several factors rather than the direct cause of the nervous breakdown. However, it is scientific to say that the habit may weaken the nervous system and indirectly affect general health, especially in pre-adolescent and early adolescent years. Probably the greatest nervous damage comes because there is often greater excess than is possible in natural sexual relations; the strain of all sexual excess is *Insanity.*

more in loss of nervous energy than of secretions. The safest advice one can give children is that the doctors agree that unnecessary touching of sexual organs has interfered with the health of many children and that those who avoid this are most likely to grow up strong in body and mind. This is the truth and practically the whole of the known truth that might have influence with young people.

Mental masturbation or "day dreaming" concerning sexual functions is probably more harmful **Mental habit.** than mechanical manipulation. It is believed to be more common in young women than in men. However, there is little reliable evidence as to the prevalence of the habit. As an educational problem, there is nothing to be done beyond informing all adolescent young people that allowing their minds to dwell on sexual affairs may interfere with nervous health, scholarship, and future efficiency in life. Hard mental and physical work and strenuous play as a daily routine will avoid or solve most such difficulties of young people.

In all dealing with this problem of young people, we must beware of overemphasis or exaggeration. **Not hopeless.** Parents and teachers should do all possible to prevent and cure the habit; but there is still hope for most young people who, in spite of warning, occasionally lapse into their old habits. Both men and women of this type have led their classes through college and won success afterwards. Probably they would have done still better if entirely free from the habit. On the other hand, men and women of neurotic inheritance combined with the habit have suffered nervous collapse during college years; and it is scientific to assume that the additional nervous strain produced by masturbation was a contributing factor. Evidently, we dare make no definite prophecy as to what will happen to one who in early life forms the habit of masturbation. There is no excuse for excessive alarm in any ordinary case; but, as we have seen, there are good reasons why parents and teachers should calmly and yet firmly help young people avoid unnatural sexual activity.

To those who must consider the problem of masturbation in boarding schools, I recommend Hime's "Schoolboys' Special Immorality."

VII

SEX-INSTRUCTION FOR EARLY ADOLESCENT YEARS

§ 27. *The Biological Foundations*

In discussing instruction for the pre-adolescent years I have stressed biological nature-study as important for the purpose of giving general knowledge of how new living things come into the world. This will develop a good attitude concerning the origin of the individual human life. In this lecture I wish to direct attention to the scientific facts which are foundations for the sexual knowledge that is important for other phases of sex-instruction during early or late adolescence.

I believe that the best introduction to advanced sex-instruction is through biological ideas which **Biological** may be presented in popular lectures **foundations.** and books; but, of course, will be best taught in courses of biological science. My own view as to the selection of materials for such biological studies is expressed in the sections on reproduction connected with the account of each animal or plant type in the "Applied Biology" and in the last chapter of the "Introduction to Biology."[1] In these books the study of life-histories of plants and animals leads up through vertebrates to mammals,

[1] Both books by M. A. and Anna N. Bigelow.

and there are a few remarks suggesting that human development is like the mammals.[1] At this point these books should be supplemented by a brief survey of the essential structure, physiology, and embryology of human reproduction.

Biological studies of human reproduction should not be coeducational in high schools or the early years of college. Mature college students who have passed through extensive biological studies, may, without apparent embarrassment, study human embryology in mixed classes; but after experience with many such groups I have begun to think that separate classes are desirable if the course is made to include all the important facts that college graduates should know concerning human reproduction. At any rate, there should be special lessons or reading dealing with detailed information that directly concerns one sex only.

Mixed classes.

I certainly do not believe in completely revamping biological science for the purposes of sex-education. It is better not to "spoil" a course by overemphasis on sex, for much of the value of biology as a basis for sex-education is the fact that sex appears gradually and naturally and far away from human relations. This impersonal approach will be lost if the course in biology seems to revolve around sex-education, for that will make sex too prominent.

Impersonal approach of biology.

[1] Sets of drawings and lantern slides for the biological introduction to sex may be obtained from the American Social Hygiene Association, 105 W. 40th St., New York City.

It is still debatable as to how much should be taught in high schools or in public lectures concerning the biological facts of human reproduction. I think that I can make my own views clearer if I discuss this first for boys, then for girls.

§ 28. *Scientific Facts for Boys*

First, it is generally agreed that boys of high-school age may profit by learning their own sexual structure by means of diagrams such as the one in Hall's "Sexual Hygiene." There is no harm, and also no gain, in minute description, especially histological.

The chief technical names of the parts of the male organs — testicle (spermary or testes), sperm duct (vas deferens), scrotum, prostate, seminal vesicles, penis, glans, prepuce (foreskin), urethra — should be taught; and the scientific dignity of these words as substitutes for vulgar words should be emphasized. In dealing with boys and young men I have noticed that these and other scientific words have a great influence on their attitude. The scientific names of the sex organs should be made part of popular vocabulary for the reason that there are no established common names corresponding to lungs, liver, stomach, arm, leg, brain, and so on for all prominent organs except the sexual. These have been left without authoritative names except in scientific language, and as a result dozens of ordinary words have been vulgarly applied and unprintable ones invented by uneducated people. Such usage of vulgar terminology is widespread, especially among men and boys. An editor of schoolbooks recently called my attention to the necessity of changing some ordinary words in certain books because in some localities the boys applied the words to sexual organs. Even the little words "nuts," "stones," "balls" accompanied by the adjective "two" mean testicles in the widespread vulgar language; and a physician told me that a college graduate used one of these words the other day when seeking medical advice concerning her baby. Here is an intolerable situation that must be improved by establishing in popular usage the dignified scientific words for the chief sexual organs. We must begin to do so by teaching the words frankly to boys of adolescent years, and by persuading parents to teach their children correctly.

Having learned the structure and names of their sexual organs, boys may easily understand the function of each part if explained in simple language. Ten or twenty minutes ought to be enough time for stating the important facts. One printed page could state them clearly. Here is the time for personal hygienic advice, especially such topics as: rules for self-control; harmful habits (see discussion of masturbation in § 26); sexual activity not necessary for health; occasional nocturnal emissions not pathological.[1]

Sex-physiology.

[1] The instructor of young men should not allow confusion to arise from the recent contention of some medical men that emissions are abnormal or unnatural because they are not known to occur in animals. Certain it is that they are adaptations to changes caused

I believe it is well for boys of adolescent years to know a few leading facts regarding female structure and function, but such knowledge is best learned from oral description by a well-balanced teacher. Diagrams and (in some schools) a demonstrated dissection of a cat or other animal will be helpful. The meaning of the ovaries as sources of the egg-cells and of the uterus as the place for development of the fertilized egg-cell should be explained in a serious way that will help boys get some fundamental ideas as to what motherhood means. Boys, moreover, should be informed concerning the existence of the periodic disturbance in the other sex, for unless they know they are sure at times to misunderstand their sisters and other girls. Professor W. S. Hall has stated the essential information in "Chums" (for boys twelve to sixteen), but his comparison of periodicity in the two sexes is not strictly accurate, for there are not in men any sexual cycles that are strictly comparable with the menstrual cycles of women.

Female organs.

by enforced sexual restraint after the seminal secretions begin with puberty. Such restraint is, of course, abnormal or unnatural if we compare with animals; but many of our acts are unnatural and not necessarily unhealthful. For instance, the sedentary life of the student or professional worker is abnormal or unnatural, but it need not be unhealthful, if hygienic adaptations are made. Likewise, seminal emissions are unnatural for primitive men or animals without sexual restraint, but this does not mean that they are unhealthful for self-controlled men. Here, as in many other cases, comparison with animals is misleading and does not teach us useful facts concerning human sexual functioning. The truth is that physicians have no evidence of harm from emissions that are not caused by voluntary activity.

It is probably best, as urged by several writers, that the life-like illustrations, some of them photographic, in books of human anatomy be kept away from boys of early adolescent age. Diagrams can be made to explain all that is necessary, and without the danger of stimulation that might come from the illustrated medical books.   *No pictures.*

The embryological facts of human biology are very impressive to boys and young men who know little of science. I believe that no other line of scientific facts is so likely to claim a serious and respectful attitude. The ideal way for giving a popular glimpse at human development is with a small series of lantern slides or photographs from embryological works. Unfortunately, there is no available popular treatment of the main facts of human development, but teachers trained in biology can easily glean the facts for the preparation of a short lecture.   *Embryology.*

Since the venereal diseases are due to microorganisms, I believe that they should be introduced in connection with the study of bacteria and other germs, either in school courses or in popular lectures. Such instruction should be very brief.   *Social diseases.*

§ 29. *Scientific Facts for Girls*

I discussed first the problem of selecting scientific facts for boys because there is little dispute as to the advisability of giving them as much scientific information as may possibly replace the vulgar knowledge that the average boy is likely to possess. I know that there are a   *Girls more innocent.*

few men and many women who will disagree with this because they believe in the absolute ignorance of their boys; but I doubt whether one healthy adolescent boy in a hundred belongs in the "innocent" class. So we need not worry much concerning any supposed danger of treating facts too frankly, provided that they are given a dignified, scientific setting. In the case of numerous adolescent girls there is certainly dense ignorance, and so there must be more difficulty in getting approval of parents and teachers concerning facts proposed for girls. Often when talking with groups of parents I have heard them say that they would like to have their boys learn the scientific truth regarding certain facts, but they feel that it would be too startling and unnecessary for their daughters. Such is the widespread feeling which must be seriously considered in all planning of advanced sex-instruction for girls. No doubt there will be much honest disagreement with the suggestions here offered.

The biological introduction based on plants and animals should be the same as for boys (§ 27).

An adolescent girl of fourteen to sixteen should know the general plan of her own sexual structure. **Structure and names.** She should know the scientific names of her organs, not because there are many vulgar names as in the case of boys, but because dignified names help attitude. Ovaries, uterus (womb), vagina, Fallopian tubes, and vulva will be sufficient. Detailed description of the external organs (vulva) might arouse curiosity that leads to exploration and irritation, and hence many women physicians think that a girl under sixteen or possibly eighteen needs only the name vulva for the external parts surrounding the entrance to the vagina.

Some books for girls perpetuate the ancient but absurd emphasis on the virginal significance of the hymen; and a recent book from a prominent publisher goes so far as to try to frighten girls into remaining chaste by stating that a physician could discover if they have been unchaste. This is far from being always true, for the structure may be congenitally absent, may sometimes remain after sexual union, or may be accidentally destroyed in childhood; and reliable physicians have stated that proving unchastity by the hymen is by no means easy. Hence, the less said about the ancient belief, the better for young women. The truth is that the hymen is a worse-than-useless relic of embryological development, and it is neither an indicator nor a dictator of morality. *An ancient belief.*

With regard to the physiology of the female organs, the following topics should be considered: The meaning of puberty as the beginning of a long fertile period of about thirty years; the nature of menstruation as a periodical process preparing the lining of the uterus for reception and attachment of an embryo if a sperm-cell meets a liberated egg-cell near an ovary, and not as a season of illness invented by the powers of *Physiology of women.*

darkness; the possibility of fertilization following sexual relations at any time during the fertile life of a woman; the essential facts of sexual relation as a method of depositing sperm-cells so that they can swim on the way to meet an egg-cell; and the nature of the close blood relationship of mother and embryo. These are physiological topics which many parents would like to have taught to their daughters of fourteen to eighteen by some careful woman or by some good book.

With regard to the social diseases and the social evil, I have long sympathized with the conservatives who hold that extremely limited knowledge is sufficient for the average girl under eighteen or twenty. No doubt that many working girls in cities need more protective knowledge than do school girls of the same age. Hall's "Life Problems" seems to me to give the important facts.

Social ills.

As in the case of boys of adolescent years, there should be enough teaching to warn against harmful habits. Such knowledge may possibly be of personal application to a few girls and it will be of use to many girls who will later as mothers or teachers have the care of small children.

Habits.

I find that many thoughtful mothers and women physicians think that girls in late adolescent years should learn from some reliable source the most general facts regarding male structure and function. Here again the strong argument is that the majority will have the care of small children. Such instruction has often

Knowledge concerning men.

been given as part of courses in biology and physiology and also in special lectures. It is certain that some parents will favor such instruction, and others will regard it as indecent to suggest that girls should have any such knowledge. There will always be some parents who will let their daughters face life-problems blindly.

Sometime in adolescent years girls should learn the scientific facts regarding mothercraft or the care of small children. This phase of the larger sex-education is rapidly attracting attention from those who are interested in practical arts education, and before many years pass it will probably be treated adequately in connection with household arts in schools and colleges. I have already referred to household arts in general as making a decided contribution to the larger sex-education which works for harmonious adjustment of the sexes in the home.

Mothercraft.

VIII

SPECIAL SEX-INSTRUCTION FOR ADOLESCENT BOYS AND YOUNG MEN

In this lecture I shall discuss a number of problems in the relations of men to women which **Methods and teachers.** ought somehow to be made clear to boys who are in transition to manhood. I can do little more than point out the lines along which it is desirable that young men should be informed and influenced; for I confess that I do not know any guaranteed pedagogical method for teaching along these lines. So far as I can now see, it seems to me that a good beginning would consist in getting the best ideas before young men by lectures, books, and personal conversations. Here more than in any other phase of sex-education the influence of personality is of great importance. Many an ordinary teacher or lecturer may well present the cold facts of biological science that help interpret sex, but one who does not by his personal qualities command the entire confidence of his hearers is worse than useless in presenting to young men such problems as those outlined in this lecture under the following subheadings: Developing young men's attitude towards womanhood; developing ideals of love and marriage; reasons for pre-marital continence; essential knowledge concerning prostitution; need of more refinement in men; dancing as a sex problem for men; dress as a sexual appeal; the problem of self-control; the mental side of a young man's sex life.

§ 30. *Developing Attitude towards Womanhood*

Many there are among the believers in the larger sex-education who feel sure that a young man's greatest safety lies in having high ideals of womanhood. I have known a number of men who passed unscathed through the storm and stress of early manhood because each of them could say, as Tennyson makes the lover confess to Princess Ida, "from earlier than I know, immersed in rich foreshadowings of the world, I loved the woman." Some of these men learned to love "the woman" in the abstract, in the dream world, perhaps as the "brushwood girl" of Kipling. Others first loved "the woman" through boyhood sweethearts. Still others came to love her through mothers who inspired them with reverence for womanhood and motherhood. *Influence of ideals.*

. . . . "Happy he
With such a mother! faith in womankind
  Beats with his blood, and trust in all things high comes easy
    to him."   (Tennyson)

But it matters little for the future purity of the boy on the threshold of manhood whether he has learned to love "the woman" in the dreamland of youth or in the very real world of life. It is simply a question of the intensity of the devotion and of the loftiness of the ideals which She has aroused within him.

Now, we of the older generation, who as parents and teachers are largely the makers of the boy's view of life, may play a very important part in developing in him a love for "the woman," a reverence for womanhood. The greatest opportunity falls to the lot of that mother whose natural gifts and education adapt her for impressing her son profoundly with appreciation of womanhood. The next greatest opportunity comes to the woman who as an instructor in school, church, or other institution comes into intimate relations that sometimes give the teacher greater influence than the mother is able or willing to exert. Finally, we must not discount the value of men's coöperation in this problem, for many a boy's attitude towards women is largely the reflection of what he has seen in his father and in other men, particularly in his teachers both secular and religious.

Who may influence boys.

Now, while the direct influence of personality is most important in this problem of developing a young man's attitude towards women, organized educational effort should not be neglected. It is important that both men and women help by encouraging young men to read good literature that unobtrusively tends to introduce them to the best in womanhood (see § 23); and by discussing with them, as opportunity offers, the higher ideals of the relationships between men and women.

§ 31. *Developing Ideals of Love and Marriage*

Closely associated with high ideals of womanhood is necessarily a pure understanding of love, even in its physical basis. While preparing this lecture I discovered that James Oliphant (in the *International Journal of Ethics*, Vol. 9, pp. 288–289, 1898) has well expressed some of the views that in a more or less unformulated shape have been in my mind for years.

"If the true preparation for love and marriage is, as I hold it to be, to learn to associate physical passion with the higher emotions developed by social sympathy — with a single-hearted devotion that demands courage, and self-sacrifice and considerate forethought and tenderness; if we wish to bind all these qualities together in the imagination of the young and clothe the conception with every attribute of beauty that fancy can devise, how can we forego the precious opportunities that lie to our hand in the persuasive witchery of art? The power that may be exercised in the formation of character by the presentment of ideal types is as yet very imperfectly utilized. Love is *par excellence* the theme of the artist, and young people will soon find this out for themselves; but there is a wide difference in the degrees of idealization, and, while we concern ourselves to exclude the grosser forms, we neglect the only effective means of accomplishing this, namely, the persistent presentation of the sentiment in its noblest examples. It is the prevalent idea that the longer we can keep

[margin note: Ideals of love in art.]

all notions of love, even in its romantic guise, out of children's heads, the better it will be for them. Surely it would be a wiser policy to fill their minds as soon as they are able to receive them, with the creations of art in which love is represented in its sublimest aspects. The youth who is familiar with the love-stories of Shakespeare, and George Eliot, and Meredith, will suffer little harm from the gilded sensualism of the Restoration drama. Let us hasten to implant the images of beauty that will keep the soul sweet and wholesome, and free from the taint of any later influences, however sordid these may be."

In the lecture on marriage as offering one of the problems for the larger sex-education (§ 12) and in the reference to general literature in § 23, I have called attention to literature which will be suggestive and useful to those who are considering the young man's attitude towards love and marriage.

§ 32. *Reasons for Pre-marital Continence of Men*

Recognizing the fact that moral considerations fail to reach many people, the following points should be emphasized in trying to show young men practical reasons why they should avoid pre-marital sexual relations.

(1) Young men ought to know that many eminent physicians and physiologists agree that it has not been Continence proved that continence injures the health and health. of men who make an effort to avoid sexual temptations. Physicians of the highest standing never advise extra-marital or immoral relations, for they are far more likely to injure health than to

improve it, and they surely injure character and reputation. On this question of continence young men should read such pamphlets as "Sexual Necessity" by Howell and Keyes; "The Young Man's Problem" and "Health and Hygiene of Sex" by Morrow; "The Physician's Answer" and "The Rational Sex Life for Men" by Exner.[1] Also, see pp. 183-190 in Geddes and Thomson's "Sex."

Dr. Exner's "Physician's Answer" is based on the following declaration which was signed by about three hundred of the foremost physicians of America:

"In view of the individual and social dangers which spring from the widespread belief that continence may be detrimental to health, and of the fact that municipal toleration of prostitution is sometimes defended on the ground that sexual indulgence is necessary, we, the undersigned, members of the medical profession, testify to our belief that continence has not been shown to be detrimental to health or virility; that there is no evidence of its being inconsistent with the highest physical, mental, and moral efficiency; and that it offers the only sure reliance for sexual health outside of marriage."

(2) It ought to be significant to young men that many men who are now in the thirties or forties look back upon their youthful errors with profound regret. Many such men testify that unfor-

[1] The first three pamphlets are published by the Society of Sanitary and Moral Prophylaxis (New York); the Exner pamphlets by the Association Press (New York).

getable immoral experiences keep them from reaching the heights of love with their wives. One of my friends, a well-known physician, recently met in his office within two or three months seven men of high standing who are now happily married, but who feel that conjugal life is short of its full æsthetic possibilities because of the ever-present remembrance of early sexual mistakes.

Psychical results of incontinence.

(3) While the above refers to the psychical effect of youthful errors, young men should learn that there is also a physical side to the same problem. Eminent physicians assert that many men have completely and permanently destroyed their sexual functions by extensive dissipations, either by masturbation or by natural relations; and that very many more have injured themselves so that perfection of the physical basis of love and marriage is impossible.

Physical results.

(4) The probability of venereal infection by premarital relations and the danger of transmission to innocent wives and children should be presented to all young men as a strong ethical appeal for continence (see § 7).

Possible diseases.

(5) The "fair play" or "square deal" appeal to young men should be based on the fact that most young men who are unchaste demand purity of the girls they claim as sisters, friends, or sweethearts; and yet they help drag down other women. An honorable man should be willing to play fairly and give purity for purity.

Purity for purity.

(6) The grave responsibility of young men whose unchastity is connected with illegitimacy or with the organized social evil should be made a strong point in appeals for pre-marital abstinence. *Responsibility.*

(7) Young men should be impressed with the idea that their sexual functions should be held sacred to affection; in other words, that sexual union is moral only as love interchange. In so far as young men may be led to this interpretation of the relation of sexuality to the best conceptions of life, there will be no danger of prostitution and there will be a guarantee of marriages that give completeness to affection. The men who are safeguarded against unchastity are those who have learned to think of love and marriage and sexual functioning as interdependent and coincident elements in the great drama of life and who feel the impossibility of their personal interest in marriage without love or in sexual union except as expression of deep affection. Such men are by no means as rare as the sensational reports of the social evil lead many people to believe. *Sexuality and affection.*

I realize that all these seven reasons for continence will fail with that large group of young men who have persuaded themselves that they will never marry and thus they shake off all responsibility such as appeals to the man who looks forward to love that culminates in marriage. No one has yet suggested any line of appeal to the men who are physically or psychi- *Some men beyond appeal.*

cally or morally so abnormal that they have no interest in the possibility of marriage; but fortunately such individuals constitute an insignificant minority.

§ 33. *Essential Knowledge Concerning Prostitution*

(1) The adolescent boy should be safeguarded by the knowledge that in every city and in most towns Safeguarding boys. there are women who for financial gain are constantly seeking to entice young men into immoral sexual relations; and that many unwary men are involuntarily entrapped, especially when influenced by alcohol.

(2) The young man should know that the selling of woman's virtue is an organized business known Prostitution as "prostitution" or "the social evil," a business. words which stand for indescribable degradation and degeneracy that no beast could possibly imitate. Moreover, the young man should be informed that all immorality is not prostitution, but that most of the immoral relations of men are purchased directly or indirectly by money or its equivalent.

(3) The young man should know that the great majority of prostitutes do not willingly undertake the Some shameful business of selling their virtue. causes of He should know that the majority have prostitution. gone downward for such reasons as follows: Many a woman has been betrayed by some detestable man who pretended to love her. Poverty has forced many other women to the first

downward step. Many are easy victims because they belong to the feeble-minded class. Others have been driven into immoral life by parents and even husbands. Still others have been drugged, and raped while insensible. A limited number have begun prostitution as "white slaves" kept as prisoners until all hope of a better life has vanished. A few have deliberately begun to accept the attentions of lewd men in order to get money for luxurious dress and finery. And relatively very few have started downward because of sexual passion such as commonly influences men. In short, every young man should be informed that most women living by prostitution have begun innocently or unwillingly; but having made one false step, society has shunned them, even near relatives have cast them off, and a career of prostitution has appeared the only way of making a living, vulgar and unspeakably sordid though it be. It is evident that the responsibility for prostitution rests almost entirely upon men. Unfortunately, society does not recognize this fact and has no way of dealing legally with both men and women found associated in houses of prostitution. At present the women arrested for prostitution are treated as criminals, while their male associates in vice are allowed to depart as if they were respectable citizens.

Tell young men these facts as to why women become prostitutes. Help them to realize that most of these women are pitiful victims of man's worse than brutal sexual passions. Then add the astounding fact that very many of the women of the underworld have short lives, their health being **Appeal to men.** undermined rapidly by dissipation, by alcohol used to bury their shame or to stimulate their flagging energies, and by the two loathsome diseases, gonorrhea and syphilis, which relatively few prostitutes escape — tell young men such facts which eminent physicians and sociologists have often verified, and there are good chances of striking sympathetic notes in their young manhood.

(4) And there is one other line of facts concerning prostitution that the developing young man should **Danger of social disease.** know well, namely, that every prostitute is likely at any time to be infected with the social diseases, and that no ordinary medical examination can prove that she will not transmit these awful diseases to men who consort with her. In fact, within an hour after most careful medical examination she may become infected by some diseased man, and then she is capable of inoculating other men. Such facts, for which the greatest of special physicians vouch, will eradicate from the young man's mind the widespread notions that prostitutes are safe if they carry a physician's certificate, or one of the official cards given in some European cities. Many a young man of sixteen to twenty has not heard that prostitutes as a class are universally dangerous as distributors of the most terrible diseases, and his education is incomplete until he knows the exact truth from reliable sources.

(5) It is not desirable that the young man should be set to read the numerous books packed with more or less sensational reports on the social evil, for these may sometimes tend toward morbidity. *Limited reading.* Any young man who is not effectively appealed to by the above facts will not be influenced by the most voluminous reports on prostitution ever published. Such reports are not useful for young men. They serve a good purpose by informing mature men and women and awakening them to the necessity of legislation, education, and other weapons with which we may fight the great black plague of social vice. For the average young man the books recommended in § 8 will give sufficient information and viewpoint.

(6) Finally, the young man of adolescent years should be made to understand his responsibility for immorality that is not prostitution, that is, extra-marital relations with his *Liaisons.* girl friends and without pecuniary considerations. He should know the probability that he will ruin a girl's life, either because illegitimacy occurs or because her reputation suffers. Even if such immoral liaisons are kept private, both persons concerned are likely in after years to regret their illicit intimacy, especially if either marries another person.

§ 34. *Need of More Refinement in Men*

While refinement is a part of general culture, it is beyond doubt an important phase of the problems for the larger sex-education. Elsewhere I have referred to the need of better understanding and better adjustment between men and women, especially in marriage. Towards such a desideratum refinement of men will contribute immensely. Many cultured women avoid marriage and many are unhappy in marriage because men, sometimes even educated men, lack refinement in manners, language, and personal habits. In fact, "lack of refinement" is altogether too mild an expression, for many men are positively crude in manners, coarse and vulgar in language, and disgusting in personal habits.

In referring to manners, I am including not only the thousand and one little customs of everyday life among refined people, but also chivalric attitude towards all women. The world has changed vastly since knighthood was in flower, but many men of to-day might well take lessons in the art of courtesy to women as practiced by the famous knights of the age of chivalry. This problem of manners will be an increasingly important one, for here in America there is growing up a generation of boys who are far from chivalrous even to their mothers and sisters; and at the same time, the industrial competition and daily association of the two sexes is making young men realize that women are simply human beings and not super beings.

Manners and chivalry.

With regard to language, I am thinking not so much of the general need of speech that is grammatically, rhetorically, and vocally polished, which no doubt determines many a woman's estimate of a man, as I have in mind the repelling effect upon sensitive women of language that is coarse, vulgar, and profane. Hence, quite apart from the effect of low language on character, I believe it worth while to work for refinement of language of young men. *Language.*

And now with reference to personal habits, including cleanliness and refinement of actions, the average women of all classes set splendid examples for men of the same groups. *Personal habits.* It seems scarcely necessary to explain in detail concerning unclean personal habits and vulgar actions. It requires no keen observer to find plenty of examples. Those who have the training of boys should lose no opportunity to impress them with the importance of refinement, and especially in all phases of their home life. It is in the most intimate life of the home that refinement of personal habits of husbands may mean much to sensitive wives.

§ 35. *Dancing as a Sex Problem for Young Men*

It is more than useless to discuss the question whether dancing ought to be eliminated from the social life of young people, for it has physical, social, and æsthetic or dramatic values which will make dancing in some form or other coextensive with human life. *Dancing not to be eliminated.*

Those who deal with adolescent boys and girls ought to have some understanding of the facts for and against dancing as it may influence the sexual control of young people, men especially. It is no longer sufficient to say, even to the young members of certain religious denominations, that "good people must not dance because it is wicked," for in this doubting age young people will ask first what we mean by the word "wicked" and then for proof that dancing is wicked. The time has come when young people must be shown the scientific reasons if we want them to avoid dancing or to dance with certain approved movements.

Young people and dancing.

It seems to be an accepted opinion among physiologists that dancing of any of the types that involve more or less closeness of contact between men and women in pairs is likely to lead to sexual stimulation that at times may be consciously recognized by normal men, but probably is not identified other than as general excitement by most women.

Dancing a sexual stimulant.

The frank admission that dancing may sometimes stimulate sexual emotions is no condemnation of dancing, as many writers seem to think. We must know first whether such emotions lead to good or harm. Sexual emotions are not in themselves wrong from any except a strictly ascetic point of view. The fact that most intelligent men who in general are frankly truthful confess that dancing may sometimes arouse sexual emotion simply raises the question whether such emotions lead

Danger no reason for condemning dancing.

directly to immoral relations with women or whether they lead, as does the best social life of men and women together, to a higher æsthetic appreciation of life as it involves the relations of the two sexes. After discussing this with many — yes, with more than a hundred — men and women, I am now convinced that dancing may have both results, depending upon the individuals. Dancing, then, has its dangers, but so have many other things that go to make up the most complete life. Eating may lead to gluttony, mountain-climbing may lead to a broken neck, swimming to drowning, music and art to sensuality, and even love is not without danger of bestial degradation. Life is full of dangers and we are constantly striving to reduce them to a minimum. So we must refuse to condemn dancing because of its admitted sexual dangers for young people, unless it can be shown that the danger is so great and so unconquerable as to outweigh all the physical, social, and æsthetic considerations in favor of the pastime.

That dancing is a strong incentive to immorality is contended by many writers. A prominent physiologist has said that "the dance is the devil's procession so far as the young man is concerned." Others have pointed to the immorality that is connected with the dance halls, and to the fact that waves of immorality of young men have often followed the annual balls given in some high schools and colleges. Contrary to the view which I formerly held, I am now in-

Dancing and immorality.

clined to think that it is not fair to charge such immoral tendencies entirely to dancing, and therefore condemn all dancing as immoral. It is no secret of sociology that similar epidemics of immorality have been known to occur in connection with Sunday-school picnics, camp meetings, expositions, political and other conventions, and religious revivals. Shall we condemn all these along with dancing on the ground that they lead to immorality? We say "no" because immorality is only an incident, not a result in these cases. Likewise, I believe that dancing is but one of several factors that have led to immorality at the time of annual balls in high school and college. These are times of general tendency towards dissipation. Regular duties are cast aside, all the hygienic rules for eating and sleeping are broken, there is unusual freedom of speech and manners, available alcohol is freely used, emotions and not reason rules — these are characteristic of the college festivals that center around grand balls. In short, at such times there is a general let-down of usual standards and a swing back towards the barbaric festival of the ancients. It is not surprising, then, that pent-up sexual instincts assert their force at such times, and dancing, if it occurs under such conditions is, of course, likely to increase the danger of moral collapse because it incites sexual emotions.

Our conclusion, then, is that it is unscientific to charge dancing with being the direct cause of immorality, when it has been only one in a series of events. The facts warrant not condemnation of dancing as something utterly bad, but rather of allowing dancing to be associated with conditions that are likely to lead to dissipation and immorality. Unless some argument other than that arising from the coincidence of dancing with dissipation and immorality is brought forward, we must conclude that dancing should be regulated and associated so that the admitted dangers will be reduced to a minimum. Recognition of the dangers will lead mature people to see the importance of supervising and regulating dancing as a phase of the social life of young people. It will lead to dancing that is improved along social and æsthetic lines.

Regulation of dancing needed.

While improvement of dancing will reduce its dangers, it will not eliminate the problem of self-control for normal young men. They must learn to understand their own emotions. They should be forewarned that others have found danger in dancing. They should know that some strong-willed men have given up dancing when they found that it made more intense the problem of sexual self-control, both mentally and physically. They should know the increased danger if dancing is associated with alcohol, vicious women, immodest dress, extreme freedom of conduct, and other morally depressing influences. Such knowledge along with general sex-education will do much to make dancing not only safe for average young men, but also helpful along social and æsthetic lines.

Self-control necessary.

With regard to the extreme dances of the past five years, those who are well informed concerning sexual problems know that many of these dances which polite society has copied from the dens of the underworld are vastly more dangerous than the standard dances.

Extreme dances.

§ 36. *Dress of Women as a Sex Problem for Men*

Some of the students of sex problems assert with great emphasis that dress is the responsible factor in the sexual immorality of many men. Accepting the probability that there is some truth in the assertion, what is the solution of the problem? Should women in general adopt a style of dress which in lines and color is as repellently ugly as the official garb of women devotees of certain religious organizations? In short, should women make their dress decidedly unobtrusive and unattractive in order that the sexual temptations of *some* men may be reduced? The answer must be an emphatic negative. We need more beauty in this life of ours, and we cannot afford to omit any beauty which women express in dress. The pity is that economic conditions so often set a limit to such expression. We must believe in making every possible application of the beauty of nature and art to human life; and beautiful dress on all women, and especially beautiful dress on attractive women, is the most important of such relations of beauty and life.

Dress and immorality.

Accepting, then, beauty of dress as worthy of

encouragement, what shall be done about its sexual attractiveness? This is a difficult question in these days with ever-changing fashions whose novelty makes extreme modes more dangerously attractive than they would be if universally adopted for a long term of years. But permanency of extreme styles or general adaptation of modest ones are absolutely impossible for the average woman of to-day. Hence, we must look forward to one extreme style following another. Young men must face the problem and fight their own battles. Like certain widespread diseases, there is constant danger of infection, and the only hope for young men is in special education as a kind of protective inoculation against temptation. This means that young men should be taught to see beauty in woman's form, face, and dress without allowing themselves to get into habits of sensual or physical emotions. Of course, for the normal young man there is sure to be more or less consciousness of emotions stimulated by the beautiful associated with women, but the individual man may train himself to turn such emotions into æsthetic or psychical lines instead of into those which are sensual, animalistic, or physical. In this connection, I have long been of the opinion that training in art appreciation, especially of sculpture, may help many men to an æsthetic attitude towards the human form.

Dress and sexual appeal.

It is well known that beauty of woman's face or form or dress has sometimes led men into immorality; but I often wonder whether such men of weak control would not have fallen sooner or later at the command of some other form of stimulation. At any rate, such men do not lead us to general conclusions, for there are many more men who have been led upward and not downward by the combined beauty of form, face, and dress of women.

While we refuse to excuse men who allow the sexual suggestiveness of women's dress to overcome their self-control, we should at the same time recognize that women have themselves to blame for much of the existing situation. I believe it is true that the average woman does not understand how dress that makes unusual exposure of the body may make a sexual appeal to men; but there is no such innocence on the part of the demi-mondes by whom many of the most dangerous styles are introduced. Perhaps women of intelligence and good standing may some day come to realize their responsibility for wearing clothing that means unusual temptation for men. However, this seems Utopian in these years when even women of the best groups are wearing equivocal dress; and so men must learn to fight their own battles against natural instincts stirred to greater intensity by dress invented to increase the trade of the women of the underworld.

Duty of women.

§ 37. *The Problem of Self-control for Young Men*

The problem of control of the insistent passions of normal young men has been unscientifically minimized by numerous writers and lecturers. It should be noted that many of these are men who have long since forgotten the storms and stresses of their early manhood, and others are women who do not know the facts indicating that the sexual instincts of young men are characteristically active, aggressive, spontaneous, and automatic, while those of women *as a rule* are passive and subject to awakening by external stimuli, especially in connection with affection. Such forgetful men and uninformed women are prone to regard the lack of control of many young men as simply due to "original sin," "innate viciousness," "bad companions," or "irresistible temptations"; and they overlook the great fact that maintaining perfect sexual control in his pre-marital years is for the average healthy young man a problem compared with which all others, including the alcoholic temptation, are of little significance. Such being the truth about young men, nothing is to be gained and much is to be lost if older people fail to take an understanding and sympathetic attitude. I question whether any young man has ever been helped through his adolescent crises by such oft-repeated assertions as that "there is no more reason that a young man should go astray than that his sister should," or, in other words, that "continence is as easy for a young man as for a girl of similar age." An observing young man will doubt such statements, and if he has had access to scientific information, he will feel sure that there has been an attempt to influence

Difference between sexes.

him by the kind of exaggeration commonly adopted by specialists in moral preachments. The plain truth is that there is a physiological "reason" or explanation, although not a justification for failure of self-control. Even if we accept the improbable statement of some writers that boys and girls are in early adolescence potentially equal in sexual instincts and assuming that they may be protected equally against vicious habits, we must not forget that every normal boy passes in early puberty through peculiar physiological changes that arouse his deepest instincts. I refer especially to the frequent occurrence of involuntary sexual tumescence and to the occasional nocturnal emissions, which processes leave the boy in no doubt whatever as to the nature, source, and desirability of sexual pleasure. Especially is this true of the automatic emissions that usually follow continence of healthy young men, for in connection with such relief of seminal pressure every nerve center of the sexual mechanism seems to be involved in the culminating nerve storm of which the awakening individual is often quite pleasurably conscious. In short, as men looking backward to their early manhood well understand, the physical sensations that come into the normal sexual experience of the adolescent boy are different only in degree of intensity from those which later are concomitants of sexual union. Such, in brief, is the physiological history of the normal adolescent boy, and one who has fallen into even most limited masturbation will

Automatic arousing of boys' instincts.

probably be still more conscious of the fact that the ordinary sequence of events in the activity of the sexual organs leads to intense excitement that has almost irresistible attractiveness.

Now, most scientifically-trained women seem to agree that there are no corresponding phenomena in the early pubertal life of the normal young woman who has good health. A limited number of mature women, some of them physicians, report having experienced in the pubertal years localized tumescence and other disturbances which made them definitely conscious of sexual instincts. However, it should be noted that most of these are known to have had a personal history including one or more such abnormalities as dysmenorrhea, uterine displacement, pathological ovaries, leucorrhea, tuberculosis, masturbation, neurasthenia, nymphomania, or other disturbances which are sufficient to account for local sexual stimulation. In short, such women are not normal. Such facts have led many physicians to the generalization that the average healthy adolescent girl does not undergo normal spontaneous changes which make her definitely conscious of the nature, source, and desirability of localized sexual pleasure. On the contrary, such consciousness commonly comes to many only as the result of stimuli arising in connection with affection.[1] Clearly it is nonsense to claim that the sexual temptations

Average young women different.

---

[1] This is really not surprising if we remember the peculiarities of human instincts mentioned in an earlier lecture (§ 3).

arising within the individual are equal for the two sexes. Potentially, girls may have passions as strong as boys, but they do not become so definitely and spontaneously conscious of their latent instincts.

Thus considering the available facts regarding the physiological reasons for the sexual tendencies of men, it seems to me that we gain nothing in trying to minimize the young man's sexual problems, for he is quite conscious that they are insistent. Far better it is that mature men who know life in its completeness should make the young man feel that his problems are not new, not insignificant, and that many another man has met and solved them in such a way as to make life more full of real happiness. Such sympathetic helpfulness will mean something to a young man, but he cannot be led far by one who in his own early experience has not learned both the strength and the mastery of the sexual instincts.

<small>Helping the young man.</small>

In another lecture I have discussed the proposition that it would be better for all concerned if women could have scientific understanding of the physiological facts concerning the sexual tendencies of men, not to make women more lenient or forgiving towards the mistakes of men, but rather to enable women to play an important part in the necessary adjustments through helpful comradeship. This last phrase will mean nothing to many people, but in many a modern home a well-informed wife has been able to lead the way to the satisfactory solution of the fundamental problems of life.

<small>Women should know.</small>

There is another and an all-important phase of the problem of teaching self-control which is commonly overlooked by those who are trying to help young men solve their greatest problems. I have in mind the need of self-control in marriage. Most writers and lecturers who emphasize the arguments for absolute self-control or continence before marriage, omit all reference to marital life. The natural inference, and one widely followed, is that the only moral duty of a young man is to control his intense desires and avoid illicit relations until sexual abandon is permitted under the license of the law and the benediction of the church. Such, I submit, is a fair conclusion for young men to draw from at least ninety per cent of the sex-education literature that is current to-day.

Self-control in marriage.

Now, I believe this is all wrong. In fact, I am so radical as to believe that the intelligent women of the world would gain more from temperance and unselfishness and delicacy of men in sexual functioning in marriage than from sexual continence before marriage. Of course, I do not propose that ideal sexual conditions in marriage may justify pre-marital incontinence, but I make this sharp contrast simply to emphasize the belief that sexual intemperance and selfishness of men in marriage causes more mental and physical suffering of women than does sexual incontinence of men before marriage, and I am not forgetting the vast problem of social diseases and prostitution.

I urge, then, that those who attempt to direct young men through the mazes of sexual life should hold up ideals not only of pre-marital continence, but also of post-nuptial temperance and harmonious adjustment between husband and wife. This post-nuptial problem is far more difficult to solve, for the intimacy of married life, especially in the earlier years, is sure to offer stimuli that are likely to make sexual instincts more insistent than those that come from celibate repression. However, self-control and temperance in marriage is no new and unattainable ideal, and harmonious adjustment of men and women in marriage is far more common than the pessimists would have us believe.

§ 38. *The Mental Side of the Young Man's Sexual Life*

Most of the discussions of the education of young men for moral living have centered around the problem of keeping him from physical sexual activity. So far as society is concerned, this is the great desideratum. So far as the individual life is concerned, it is important that self-control should extend to mental imagery. Professors Geddes and Thomson have well said, in "Sex," that "while anatomical chastity is a moral achievement, it is not the deepest virtue. The incisive declaration: 'Whosoever looketh on a woman to lust after her hath committed adultery with her already in his heart' expresses an even more searching standard, and modern science brings home

Effect of mental imagery.

SEX–INSTRUCTION FOR BOYS AND MEN 183

to us the radical importance of our reflex thought and deep-down impulses, which appear to bulk largely in molding our lives and the lives of those who may spring from us." In language adapted to the understanding of average young men, this idea should be emphasized.

In the opinion of some physiologists the greatest harm done to the individual who has long been a victim of masturbation is in the centering of the attention on imaginary sexual situations. This is especially true of mental masturbation. Hence, the relation of masturbation to the possible establishment of a disordered mental state should be known by adolescent boys and young men.

It appears from the experience of many men that strenuous work and play are the only efficient weapons for driving sexual images into the background of the mind. This ap- plies not only to sordid and lewd thoughts of unchaste sexual situations, but also to the mental images that are inevitably associated with the purest affection and which should be trained to obey when calm reason so orders. *Control of thoughts.*

The following literature will be especially helpful to young men: W. S. Hall's "Sexual Hygiene for Men," or his "Sexual Knowledge"; Exner's "The Rational Sex Life for Men"; Morrow's "The Young Man's Problem," and "Health and Hygiene of Sex for College Students"; King's "Fight for Character" (Y.M.C.A.); and the chapter on Ethics of Sex in "Sex" by Geddes and Thomson.

IX

SPECIAL SEX-INSTRUCTION FOR MATURING YOUNG WOMEN

It was my original plan to make this lecture parallel with the preceding one for young men, but much discussion with parents and with scientifically trained women whose suggestions and criticisms I value has shown me that there is no consensus of opinion as to what should be taught to young women between eighteen and twenty-two years of age. I have found many fathers and mothers who think that their boys of fourteen or fifteen should be informed as suggested in the preceding lecture; but concerning some of the facts for boys these same parents were doubtful whether their daughters ought to know before twenty, and some of them have said twenty-five and even thirty. Some of them have said that they see no reason why an unmarried young woman of the protected group should know much more than a very limited amount of personal hygiene; but most of these people were decidedly hazy as to how the young woman about to marry may be sure of getting belated knowledge. In short, all along the line I have found intelligent

Parents would limit knowledge of daughters.

parents and others who believe in very thorough sex-instruction for boys, but that "nice" girls should be kept as ignorant and innocent as possible. With such disagreement existing, it is evidently not possible to make such specific recommendations as have been made for boys.

§ 39. *The Young Woman's Attitude towards Manhood*

Among those who agree heartily with the proposition that by education the young man's attitude towards womanhood (§ 30) should be cultivated I find, to my surprise, many who object to any parallel attempt to influence young woman's ideals of manhood. I say that I am surprised because it has long seemed to me that many of the faults of men are largely traceable to the fact that women as a sex have not been able to hold a high standard for manhood; and, therefore, I wonder when some thinking women question the desirability of trying to influence young women by organized instruction. Of course, we must not forget that before the coming of the economic and social freedom of women there were very few of them who were able to maintain a stand for their ideals of manhood; but this is no longer true in a great and rapidly increasing group of the individualized and educated classes. Therefore, it seems clear that if the better groups of women want a higher type of manhood capable of better adjustment in marriage, it is important that they consider

Women should have ideals.

ways and means of molding the minds of young women with reference to ideal manhood.

Occasionally I have met a strange view of life in some men and women who have grown pessimistic from revelations concerning the sexual-social problems and who think that true manhood is so rare that emphasizing it with young women will lead to ideals that can rarely be realized in actual life; and therefore, for women so influenced there will be increasing discontent and disappointment in marriage or deliberate celibacy. No doubt this is in part true, as witness the many highly educated women who have written or said that there seem to be few attractive marriageable men of their own age. However, it is rare indeed that such women say that life would have meant more without the higher education and its resulting ideals that have stood in the way of marriage such as might be happy for uneducated women. This is in line with the fact that many cultivated men and women find that education has given unattained ideals and unsatisfied ambitions and strenuous life and disappointments, but it is rare that they long for the care-free and animal-like happiness of the tropical savage. We must remember that education gives us keener feeling for life's pains, but it also compensates by giving soul-satisfying appreciation of its joys. So it seems reasonable to believe that while educating young women to believe in and demand a higher ideal of manhood in its natural relations to womanhood will certainly make disappoint-

Ideals and disappointment.

ments more heart-pressing for some, it will just as surely make realization the supreme happiness of others. And as adjustment of manhood and womanhood through the larger sex-education becomes more and more abundant and more and more perfected, the sum total of human happiness will increase.

Looking thus towards the ultimate good, I must refuse to accept the hopeless and depressing view that all young women should be kept ignorant of their relation to men and life in order that the absence of ideals of manhood may protect some women against possible disappointment by men.

§ 40. *The Young Woman's Attitude towards Love and Marriage*

In the preceding lecture to the parents and teachers of young men I emphasized the importance of developing the young man's ideals of love and marriage primarily because such ideals have so often helped men morally in character-formation and character-protection. feel sure that this is not the chief reason why the ideals of young women should be developed along parallel lines. On the contrary, it seems to me that those representative women are right who think that the first reason why ideals of young women should be influenced is that there is need of a radical change in the attitude of a very common type of young women who are flippant and disrespectful concerning love and marriage, and whose influence on the

Reasons not same as for men.

morals of men is decidedly bad because they often give unguided young men their first and strongest impressions concerning women. A second reason, which is equally applicable to both sexes, is that advance understanding of the relations of love and marriage is likely to lead to happy and satisfactory adjustment in marriage.

Perhaps the flippant and disrespectful attitude concerning affairs of the heart develops in many young women because they do not consciously feel in advance of experience the demand for affection which comes so naturally and spontaneously to many, possibly to all, normal young men whose views of life have not been artificially twisted. I fully realize the treacherous nature of the ground on which walks one who tries to compare the two sexes concerning their relative attitudes towards love, but certain it is that the novelist's descriptions of men as the leaders and aggressors in love is not fiction but the common fact of real life. Man's tendency towards leadership in love is not scientifically explained by any superficial assumption that established social conventions have repressed an original spontaneity of women. On the contrary, there are the best of physiological and psychological reasons for believing that the social conventions have arisen as an expression of masculine aggressiveness and natural tendency towards leadership in affairs of the heart. The accepted fact is that many young women have no understanding of or demand for affection until experience

Men naturally lead in love.

has taught them its place in life. In the records of real life, as well as in fiction, many a young woman's possibilities of happiness have been lost because she did not understand herself when love came into her experience.

Another side to the problem of the young woman's relation to love and marriage is brought to our attention by the lamentable fact that many wives lose interest in devoted husbands when the children come. *Affection in marriage.* This is probably true in at least half the families; and many matrimonial disharmonies are the result. This is really one of the greatest problems of marriage which cultured women should consider seriously; for even more than in most other sex problems, it is one for the solution of which women are in a position to take the leading part. This problem is especially important in these days when the household inefficiency, personal extravagance, and desire for social position of numerous young women of eighteen to thirty are having an enormous influence in advancing the age of marriage because many of the best types of young men pause and consider seriously the impossibility of adjusting a small salary to the ideas of their women friends as to what is the minimum of a family budget. Add to such facts a growing pessimism of young men regarding inconstant affections of wives with children, and the need of special educational attack is evident.

From whatever side we look at the question whether the larger sex-education should somehow try to mold the ideals of young women with regard to love and marriage, we see reasons why parents should encourage their maturing daughters to get some advance understanding of such relation. If parents are themselves unable to help their daughters to this understanding, they can at least exert great influence by their own attitude, and they can approve the reading of books, and perhaps there may be opportunity for hearing lectures by women who understand life.

The duty of parents.

With regard to good literature that will help in this line, there are chapters in many of the books mentioned at the end of this lecture, and in more or less indirect form in the general literature suggested in the preceding lectures concerning young men, and in § 12 which deals with the general educational problem of marriage.

Books.

§ 41. *Reasons for Pre-marital Continence of Women*

Many women who have lived protected lives have declared themselves unable to understand why a young woman should need reasons for pre-marital continence; and these women are probably right so far as the great majority of the daughters of families in good social conditions are concerned. As pointed out in earlier lectures, there is abundant evidence that the average adolescent girl who is protected against external sexual stimuli and influenced constantly by the prevailing ideals which demand chastity of women, is not likely to need any argu-

Many women do not need reasons.

ments why she should avoid pre-marital incontinence. Moreover, there seems to be little danger that the average girl with good social environment will ever question her ideals of chastity unless under the stress of overwhelming affection; in other words, there is little possibility that such women will be interested in the strictly mechanical, non-affectionate, and unsentimental sexual relations which must inevitably characterize the common prostitution of men.

Note that I am referring to the average young woman in good social environment, and for the moment omitting the vast class of so- called "unprotected" girls. Moreover, I am speaking of the "average," and I am not forgetting that medical journals and books record many exceptions. Nevertheless, we must not be misled by medical literature, for naturally the physician sees the women whose lack of health leads them to seek professional advice, and it is well known that in sexual lines women commonly become decidedly unhealthy before they consult physicians. As testimony concerning the average normal women, I have the greatest confidence in the statements of thoughtful women with sound scientific attitude; and such are my authority for the view that maintaining pre-marital continence is not one of the serious problems for the average young woman with good domestic and social environment.

Unprotected girls.

Now, while I admit in advance that the problem of pre-marital continence is not of great significance in the personal lives of the great majority of the type of women who are likely to hear or read this lecture, I do believe that this is the type of women who ought to think over the problem as it concerns the atypical girl of good social groups and the "unprotected" girl of more unfortunate groups. I cannot see, therefore, why it is not best and safest that all girls should learn from parents or reliable books or teachers the main reasons for pre-marital chastity.

The atypical girls of good social groups who need guidance regarding pre-marital continence are of two types: either one with intensive sexuality which is often modifiable by medical or surgical treatment; or one of probably normal instincts but with radical sexual philosophy. The first type needs not only emphatic instruction regarding continence, but more often medical help, either for general health or for correction of localized sexual disturbance. The second type must be treated exactly as suggested for young men, because they are the women whose anarchistic repudiation of laws and convention in general has led to their acceptance of a *single* standard of morality for men and women, but one of freedom from monogamic ideals. This type of women, long well known in the student groups of Paris and in Russian universities, is becoming more and more evident in America, especially among some well-educated young women who have dropped their ideals of chastity because they have found attractiveness in more or less superficial studies of radical socialism. Many of these

The girl who needs help.

radical women frankly say that they would like to marry the "right man," but failing to find that rare species, they claim their right to sexual freedom in more or less capricious liaisons. Others of these women are so highly individualized that marriage is beneath their contempt, either because it will "interfere with a career" or because the legal aspects and ecclesiastical ceremonies still suggest the old-time subjection of the wife to the husband. Women who are in a position to know from personal knowledge of radical people declare that there are still relatively few educated women who deliberately cut loose from monogamic standards; and that they are most commonly found among certain intimate and unconventional groups of students and professional workers, especially those who are united in "Bohemian life" by artistic or literary interests. But while such sexually anarchistic women are not common in America, there is reason for fearing that, unless some unexpected check comes to this undercurrent towards sexual freedom, it may be found ten or twenty years hence that a surprisingly large number, but *never a majority*, of unmarried young women have fallen into the sexual promiscuity that is so common among unmarried men of the same ages.

Chief of the influences that lead a certain number of well-educated young women towards sexual freedom is radical printed matter. We are now getting in America a wide distribution of bold literature of the "free love" type, some of it with a scientific superficiality that will Radical sex literature.

convince many beginners in the study of sexual problems. Much of this literature is translation or adaptation of books and articles by European authors; and I have previously remarked that abroad the ideals of sexual morality — and judging from the Great War, of morality in other lines — is frankly quite different from that upheld here. But some of this radical literature is American in origin. In addition to certain books and pamphlets, which might be advertised by giving names, I think of two New York medical journals, with a popular circulation, edited by a successful but much criticized physician, which rarely publish an issue without frank approval and even arguments for extra-marital relations other than prostitution, particularly for those who for one reason or another, unwelcome or voluntary, are leading celibate lives. The influence of such writings on young women who are inclined towards radicalism in all things is probably enormous, and it is unfortunate that vigorous opposition literature is not published and widely circulated.

In conclusion, it is clear that the problem of premarital continence is not limited to young men, for the "unprotected" girl from a low-grade home and environment, and the uninformed girl from the best of homes, and the radical girl from the most educated circles may, innocently or deliberately, select the pathway to unchastity. For these kinds of young women the educational problem is the same as for young men. They should have essentially the same in-

Same instruction as for men.

struction. And, in the case of both sexes, it is only by contrasting the good and evil that education can point out the worth-whileness of chastity.

There is a special aspect of the problem of pre-marital chastity of men that young women should understand, and that is their indirect responsibility for the unchastity of many men. In discussing dancing (§35) and extreme dress (§36), it has been indicated that women as a sex have a tremendous responsibility for the temptations of men. The same is true in the case of flirting or more extreme familiarities with men. However sure a young woman may feel of her own power of self-control, she should not consider lightly her possible part in a chain of events which may lead men to unchastity with other women. Many a man driven into the white heat of passion by thoughtless or deliberate acts of a pure girl has gone direct to seek relief of tension in the underworld. Of course, the girl in this case is not directly responsible for the downfall of the man; but I wonder if there is not moral, if not legal, responsibility for one who knowingly leads or helps another to the brink of a precipice from which he voluntarily falls. *Indirect responsibility.*

I am perfectly well aware that many good people will be horrified by the very suggestion that young women should be taught their responsibility for their men associates. Some will declare that the advocates of sex-education propose to destroy the innocence and romance in young women's lives. Others of the horrified ones will remain complacent because they believe that unchastity is caused by "innate depravity" of men. I am sorry to disagree with such people who are sincere, but the established facts point clearly to the conclusion that it is the duty of the mothers and teachers of girls to make them understand their relations to men and their responsibility for helping young men avoid sexual temptations. This is necessary when innocence stands in the way of the maximum safety and happiness of young people.

§ 42. *Need of Optimistic and Æsthetic Views of Sex by Women*

The most significant point in the sex-education movement at present is the fact that numerous women of the most intelligent groups are tending rapidly towards accepting an optimistic and æsthetic view of sexual relationships so far as these are normal and ethical and guided by affection. However, this higher philosophy of sexual life is still very far from being universal among educated women, and it is probably true that to the great majority of them sexuality has no æsthetic meaning but is simply a very troublesome physical function and an animal method for perpetuating the human species. That such an attitude should be common is not surprising, for in recent years numerous educated women have gained abundant information concerning abnormal sexuality, while very few have caught glimpses of the higher possibilities of the sexual

Many women pessimistic concerning sexuality.

functions. The truth is that it has been and still is difficult for most women to get well-balanced knowledge of sexual normality. There are hundreds of books and pamphlets that deal with amazing boldness with the sexual mistakes of human life, but there is not in general circulation to-day any printed matter which deals with normal sexual life with anything like the frankness and directness that is common in widely circulated literature on social vice and its concomitant diseases. Likewise, it is difficult for women to get the true view of sexual life from personal sources, for the vulgar side of sexuality is the one usually discussed by most people, some of whom revel in obscenity, some have had personal experiences that have caused ineradicable bitterness, and some more or less sincerely believe that knowledge of vice is of value as a safeguard or an antidote. The bright side of the sexual story is rarely told in conversation, either because it is unfamiliar or because it is the sacred secret between pairs of individuals who together have found life in all its completeness.

Fortunately, this depressing emphasis on sexual abnormality is beginning to disappear, and we see sure signs of coming attention to sexual health rather than to disease and to purity rather than to vice. Leading women are beginning to give, through the impersonal medium of science and general literature, some definite and helpful testimony concerning the pathway to the essential good that is bound up in sexuality.

Æsthetic outlook.

It is especially important that young women of culture should be helped to this point of view, and as far as possible before they learn much concerning the dark problems that have originated from failure to keep sexual functions sacred to affection and possible parenthood. The educated women of to-day who have acquired and retained faith in the essential goodness of human sexual possibilities, and who at the same time have an understanding of the mistakes that weak humans are wont to make, are sure to play a most important part as teachers and mothers and leaders in the movement which is already guiding numerous intelligent men and women to a purified and noble view of the sexual relationships. As I see the big problems that demand sex-education, the future will depend largely upon the attitude of women. It is an essential part of the feministic movement. In the past there have been many alarming signs of a destructive sex antagonism that charged men with full responsibility for existing sex problems. But the advance guards of feminism are beginning to recognize that there are all-essential relationships between the sexes, and that only in sex coöperation can there be any permanent solution of the great questions. It is a great advance from the sex hostility of Christabel Pankhurst's "Plain Facts on a Great Evil" to the co-working attitude of Louise Creighton's "Social Disease and How to Fight It," of Olive Schreiner's "Woman and Labor," of Ellen Key's "Love and Marriage," and of Gascoigne

Hartley's "Truth About Woman," all of which give us hope that women with optimistic and æsthetic interpretation of sex are coming to take the lead towards a better understanding of the relations of sex and life.

§ 43. *Other Problems for Young Women*

Concerning several other problems that have been discussed with special reference to young men, it seems best that all young women should be informed sometime between sixteen and twenty-two, the age limit depending upon maturity of the individual, home life, and social environment.

With regard to prostitution, it seems important that girls should know the essential facts recommended in the lecture concerning boys. The "unprotected" girl of low-grade environment will often need some of this knowledge before she is fourteen (and in some cases, even twelve) years old. On the other hand, the average "protected" girl need not know until several years later. It seems possible that too early familiarity with the existence of sexual vice might tend to make some young women accept it as part of the established order of things; and, hence, the girl whose environment is protective and whose moral training has been complete will be perfectly safe without knowledge of vice and will be more likely to take an opposition attitude if she learns the facts concerning prostitution when she is approaching maturity. Even then the essential information should be given

_{Prostitution.}

in such a way that the young woman will see the gravity of the social situation and, at the same time, not develop a spirit of sex hostility. Here, again, I must recommend Louise Creighton's "Social Disease and How to Fight It" as not only pointing out the nature of the great evil, but also recognizing that the existing situation can never be improved except by the sympathetic coöperation of the best men and women.

With regard to dancing, young girls should be taught that certain forms of this exercise are not approved by the most refined people. Before maturity, they should not know the physiological reason for this disapproval. In fact, I know many men and women who think it best that most women, even mature, should not have their attention called to the sexual dangers of dancing. For my part, I cannot see how women with such ignorance can coöperate with the best men in reducing the admitted dangers to a minimum.

Dancing.

With regard to dress as a sexual problem, some mothers think they can handle the problem with their young daughters by emphasizing modesty and without further explanation; but the drawing power of fashions is so great that most young women are quick to revise their ideas of modesty to suit the latest style. Is it too much to hope that large numbers of young women would accept such facts as were stated in the lecture for young men (§ 36), and would be sincere enough to dress so that their attractiveness may appeal more

Dress.

to the æsthetic and less to the physical natures of men?

In this lecture concerning the special teaching of young women, I have attempted nothing more than an outline of the impressions that I have gained from books and from representative women who are interested in the larger sex-education. *Merely a man's views.* I have not tried to make the discussion as extensive as that for young men, first, because I cannot believe that young women in general need so much special instruction; and, second, because only women can adequately advise concerning the sex-educational problems of young women. However, since the women who might be expected to know the truth about women have failed to agree on so many points, it may be worth while for a man to contribute some suggestions based on the most scientific information offered by some very reliable women.

Among the books which touch the special problems for young women, I am most favorably impressed by the following: Hall's "Life Problems" in the first thirty-two pages is adapted *Books.* for girls of twelve to fourteen, and the remainder for older girls. Some parents are not enthusiastic about the story form, but the facts are well selected and presented. The last chapter of Smith's "Three Gifts of Life" is worth reading, but the first chapters are unscientific. For almost mature young women, there are chapters of Rummel's "Womanhood and Its Development," of Wood-Allen's "What a Young

Woman Should Know," of Lowry's "Herself," and of Galbraith's "Four Epochs of a Woman's Life." The last two are decidedly medical in point of view. The part for girls in Scharlieb and Sibley's "Youth and Sex," and some chapters of March's "Towards Racial Health," are good. The last two chapters of Geddes and Thomson's "Sex" will be appreciated by many intellectual young women. Hepburn's sentimental little story "The Perfect Gift" (Crist Co., 3¢) has helped many young people improve their æsthetic outlook. There are some helpful ideas in Henderson's "What It Is To Be Educated" (Houghton Mifflin Co.). While disagreeing (§ 46) with Dr. Richard Cabot's extreme emphasis on a mystical religious solution for problems of sex, I recognize that many young women have been helped by his "The Christian Approach to Social Morality" (Y.W.C.A.), and by his "What Men Live By."

X

CRITICISMS OF SEX-EDUCATION

In the preceding lectures we have considered the arguments for sex-instruction. It will now be helpful to review some of the writings of those who oppose or at least point out the defects of the commonly accepted plan of sex-instruction. None of those writers whom I shall quote is known to be absolutely opposed to all sex-instruction, but some of them would limit the instruction so much that there would be little hope of the general movement having an important influence.

§ 44. *A Plea for Reticence Concerning Sex*

Miss Agnes Repplier, the distinguished essayist, discusses in the *Atlantic Monthly* (March, 1914) the plain speech on sex topics that are before the public to-day. While she holds no brief for "the conspiracy of silence," which she admits was "a menace in its day," she maintains that "the breaking of silence need not imply the opening of the flood-gates of speech." She goes on to say:

Agnes Repplier.

"It was never meant by those who first cautiously advised a clearer understanding of sexual relations and hygienic rules that everybody should chatter freely respecting these grave issues; that teachers, lecturers, novelists, story-writers, militants, dramatists, social workers, and magazine editors should copiously impart all they know, or assume they know, to the world. The lack of restraint, the lack of balance, the lack of soberness and common sense were never more apparent than in the obsession of sex which has set us all ababbling about matters once excluded from the amenities of conversation.

Present frankness.

"Knowledge is the cry. Crude, undigested knowledge, without limit and without reserve. Give it to boys, give it to girls, give it to children. No other force is taken account of by the visionaries who — in defiance, or in ignorance of history — believe that evil understood is evil conquered.

"We hear too much about the thirst for knowledge from people keen to quench it. Dr. Edward L. Keyes, president of the Society of Sanitary and Moral Prophylaxis, advocates the teaching of sex-hygiene to children, because he thinks that it is the kind of information that children are eagerly seeking. 'What is this topic,' he asks, 'that all these little ones are questioning over, mulling over, fidgeting over, worrying over? Ask your own memories.'

"I do ask my memory in vain for the answer Dr. Keyes anticipates. A child's life is so full, and everything that enters it seems of supreme importance. I fidgeted over my hair which would not curl. I worried over my examples which never came out right. I mulled (though unacquainted with the word) over every piece of sewing put into my incapable fingers, which could not be trained to hold a needle. I imagined I was stolen by brigands, and became — by virtue and intelligence — spouse of a patriotic outlaw in

One child's life.

a frontierless land. I asked artless questions which brought me into discredit with my teachers, as, for example, who 'massacred' St. Bartholomew. But vital facts, the great laws of propagation, were matters of but casual concern crowded out of my life and out of my companions' lives (in a convent boarding-school) by the more stirring happenings of every day. How could we fidget over obstetrics when we were learning to skate, and our very dreams were a medley of ice and bumps? How could we worry over 'natural laws' in the face of a tyrannical interdict which lessened our chances of breaking our necks by forbidding us to coast down a hill covered with trees? The children to be pitied, the children whose minds become infected with unwholesome curiosity are those who lack cheerful recreation, religious teaching, and the fine corrective of work. A playground or a swimming pool will do more to keep them mentally and morally sound than scores of lectures on sex-hygiene.

"The world is wide, and a great deal is happening in it. I do not plead for ignorance, but for the gradual and harmonious broadening of the field of knowledge, and for a more careful consideration of ways and means. There are subjects which may be taught in class, and subjects which commend themselves to individual teaching. There are topics which admit of *plein-air* handling, and topics which civilized man, as apart from his artless brother of the jungles, has veiled with reticence. There are truths which may be, and should be, privately imparted by a father, a mother, family doctor, or an experienced teacher; but which young people cannot advantageously acquire from the platform, the stage, the moving picture gallery, the novel or the ubiquitous monthly magazine."

Personal teaching approved.

There is much in Miss Repplier's paragraphs which will win hearty approval from those who have come to believe, as advocated throughout this series of lectures, in conservative teaching of sex-hygiene and a larger outlook for sex-education.

No doubt there has been too great a loss of a certain kind of reticence and a substitution of crude frankness, but it has not been caused by the sex-education movement. On the contrary, there are two evident sources of the plain speech of which Miss Repplier and others have complained: First, the commercializing of sex by novelists, dramatists, theater managers, and publishers — many of whom are reaping a golden harvest and few of whom have any sincere interest in promulgating sexual information to any end except their own pocketbooks. Second, the development of the feminist movement which has its deepest foundation in the age-old sexual misunderstandings of women by men, and which has led on and on into social and political complications of gravest significance. The very nature of the feminist revolt from masculine domination made plain speaking on sex matters inevitable.

Current frankness not due to sex-education.

Neither of these sources of plain speech need give us cause for alarm, for a great reaction is already coming. The sensationalism of sexual revelations has had its day, and the intelligent public is recovering its balance. A lurid novel or play resembling "Damaged Goods" or "The House of Bondage"

Reaction against sensational frankness.

or certain vice-commission reports would not now be accepted by some prominent publishers who recently would not have hesitated to seize a first-class commercial opportunity in this line. The fact is that sexual sensationalism has ceased to pay because the intelligent public knows the main facts and has become disgusted with crude frankness that amounts to lasciviousness. On the side of feminism there is hope in the widespread disgust with Cristabel Pankhurst's "Plain Facts on a Great Evil" as compared with the very general approval of Louise Creighton's polished masterpiece, "The Social Evil and How to Fight It." This represents exactly the present attitude of numerous men and women who calmly discuss together the great problems of life fearlessly and without any elements of lasciviousness such as some people seem to think is necessarily associated with either unsexual or bisexual discussion of sex problems.

Miss Repplier's description of her own lack of youthful interest in things sexual is of value simply as applied to a limited number of extra-protected girls. Her experience teaches us nothing regarding boys or even girls under average conditions. We know beyond any doubt that average children in or near adolescence do seek the kind of information that Miss Repplier denies having thought about. It is not "pressed relentlessly upon their attention" by teachers, but by instinct and by environment. Playground and swimming pools and religious influence and work

Not a typical case.

are all helpful in our dealings with young people, but all together they are inadequate without some information concerning sex.

Finally, Miss Repplier, like so many other critics of sex-instruction, has in mind only the physical consequences of wrong-doing. Here again is the influence of the pioneer sex-hygiene. However, she pleads for the "gradual and harmonious broadening of the field of knowledge and for a more careful consideration of ways and means" for sex-instruction. This makes us believe that she will favor the larger sex-education which gives a place to "the cheerful recreation, the religious teaching, the childish virtues, the youthful virtues, the wholesome preoccupation," as well as essential knowledge of physical facts; and all as factors in preparing young people consciously and unconsciously to face the inevitable problems of sex. On the whole, we must regard Miss Repplier's discussion as a helpful contribution to the saner aspects of sex-education.

Conclusion.

§ 45. *A Plea for Religious Approach to Sex-instruction*

Another prominent author who does not agree with the current tendencies of sex-instruction is Cosmo Hamilton in his little book entitled "A Plea for the Younger Generation" (Doran Co.). He agrees with the sex-education writers that children should be instructed

Cosmo Hamilton.

early, and as far as possible by their parents; but he wholly disagrees with the method of biological introduction. He would have parents go straight to the heart of the matter and tell the child, as simply and truly as can be, just how he came into the world. And he would fill the teaching with reverence by using as an illustration the birth of the babe of Bethlehem. Referring to those who in recent years have been working for a scientific introduction to sex-education, Mr. Hamilton says:

"I think that these professors and scientists are wasting their time, and I have written this small volume not only in order to make a plea for the younger generation as to the way in which they shall be taught sex truths, but also in order, if possible, to prove to the advanced thinkers of the day that it is not old-fashioned to beg that God may be put back into the lives of His children, but a thing of urgent and vital importance. Without faith the new generation is like a city built on sand. Without the discipline and the inspiration of God the young boys and girls who will all too soon be standing in our shoes will go through life with hungry souls, with nothing to live up to, and very little to live for." *[Religious appeal.]*

All this is very good so far as it appeals to the religious type of mind, but Mr. Hamilton seems to forget that vast numbers of people cannot be approached from this point of view. How can the illustration of the Christ-child help those who do not accept certain orthodox religious beliefs? *[Many not reached by religious appeal.]*

§ 46. *The Conflict between Sex-hygiene and Sex-ethics*

It has been said in an earlier lecture that several writers have declared that sex-ethics and sex-hygiene are essentially conflicting and should not be associated in teaching; that is to say, that hygienic facts should not be taught with the hope of improving morals. Most prominent of those who have de-
Richard Cabot. clared that hygienic and moral teaching should be dissociated is Dr. Richard C. Cabot, of Boston. I shall give in this lecture attention to his writings because they have tended to introduce confusion by critical attention to certain weak details and unessentials in the original suggestions for sex-education, and by wrongly assuming that the original "sex-hygiene" was aimed at improved morals, whereas it was aimed directly at health. In a paper entitled "Consecration of the Affections (often misnamed 'Sex-hygiene')," read at the fifth (1911) Congress of the American School Hygiene Association, Dr. Cabot attacked the kind of sex-instruction that is limited to sex-hygiene. He has later returned to the attack on many occasions. I shall quote a number of his paragraphs and follow each with a discussion of its contents.

(1) "The straight, right action in matters of human affection has nothing to do with hygiene. For
Hygiene and conduct. hygiene has no words to proclaim as to why you and I should behave ourselves. Hygiene has the right and the duty to make clear the perverted and the diseased consequences of certain errors. But these consequences

are far from constant. . . . Let us disabuse our minds, then, of the idea that there are always bad physical consequences of mistake, error, or sin in this [sex] field, and that those consequences are reasons for behaving ourselves. But even if there were such consequences, I think it even more mischievous for us to preach a morality based upon them."

That hygienic knowledge makes many people control their sexual selves is beyond dispute. Because the consequences of sexual error are far from constant is a weak argument against pointing out possible results. The consequences from pistols are far from constant, and yet I have no doubt that Dr. Cabot would teach small boys the danger of shooting themselves and other people.

The last quoted sentence suggests Dr. Cabot's whole basis of contention against sex-hygiene. He seems to have inferred from the earlier papers, especially those by Dr. Morrow, that the hygiene of sex is to be taught as an approach to morality. On the contrary, the truth is that the aim of most of the first leaders in sex-instruction was to teach hygiene and ethics primarily in order to improve health. Dr. Morrow and others believed that hygienic teaching would secondarily react on sexual morality; but the original aim of the Society of Sanitary and Moral Prophylaxis was to limit the spread of venereal disease by sanitary, moral, and legal means. In other words, moral appeals were to aid in checking disease, and knowledge of disease

Hygiene and ethics for health.

was not claimed to improve morality, although such knowledge might react against immorality. It is this misunderstanding or overlooking of the real reasons for teaching concerning sex health that seems to have led Dr. Cabot into apparent opposition to the general movement for sex-instruction. One infers from all his lectures that he believes it good to teach hygiene for health, ethics for morality, and biology for science; but that these should not be correlated because to him they are unrelated. It seems to me that he has simply been misled by the overenthusiasm of some of the first writers on sex-hygiene and by the widespread use of that limited term instead of sex-education.

Is sex-hygiene immoral? (2) "Now I say that the preaching about sex-hygiene that is going on in recent books and in the periodical press is immoral in its tendency. It is like saying, 'Don't lie, for if you do, you won't sleep at night, and insomnia is bad for the health.'"

If insomnia often follows lying, then it should be taught as *one* reason why falsehoods should be avoided. This is not opposed to ethical teaching, for at the same time we can teach the other reasons for not telling lies. Likewise, sex-hygiene offers certain reasons for conduct and may be supplemented by sex-ethics.

(3) "The attempts to consecrate affection and to safeguard morality by teaching in public or private schools what is called 'sex-hygiene' will, I believe,

prove a failure. I have very little confidence in the restraining or inspiring value of information, as such. I have seen too much of its powerlessness in medical men and students. No one knows so much of the harm of morphine as the physicians do, yet there are more cases of morphine habit among physicians than among any less informed profession. It is, of course, easy to make young children familiar with the facts of maternity and birth. Compared to the ordinary methods of concealment and lying by parents to children about these matters this is doubtless an improvement, but it does almost nothing to meet the moral problems of sex which come up later in the child's life. One may know all about maternity, without knowing anything of the difficulties and dangers of sex. Many have thought that by thorough teaching of the physiology of reproduction in plants and animals we can anticipate and to a considerable extent prevent the dangers and temptations referred to above."

Information and morality.

It is not proposed "to consecrate affection" or "to safeguard morality" by hygienic knowledge; but simply to protect health. Of course, information will not restrain everybody; but if physicians did not know the dangers of morphine many more would be victims of the drug. Dr. Cabot overlooks the fact that physicians know how to use and obtain morphine, while other professional men do not. Teaching concerning maternity and birth will not directly meet the moral problems of sex, but it will help develop an attitude, "a consecration of the affections," that will guard against the dangers of sex. Such teaching to children is only one of many steps in the scheme of sex-education. No responsible advocate of sex-instruction claims that teaching children concerning the reproduction of animals and plants does anticipate and prevent sexual temptations; but it is a foundation for practical knowledge of human sex problems. I have elsewhere referred to the effect of such studies on attitude.

(4) "The positive moral qualities which make us immune to the dangers of sex are obtainable not through warnings as to dangers, but through the more positive activities just alluded to. All that is most practical and successful in this field of endeavor may be summarized as the *contagion of personality, human or divine.* What is it that keeps any of us straight unless it is the contagion of the highest personalities whom we have known, in man and God?"

Contagion of personality.

We must admit that, perhaps, "positive moral qualities" are not obtainable through warnings, but in this pragmatic age we must have good social results gained by any honorable means. Many people are kept from crime by warnings of the law. Of course, this is not a "positive moral" result for the unethical individual who must be restrained by fear of legal consequences, but we do not worry about the individual when society gains. Likewise, a man kept from sexual promiscuity by fear of disease is not more positively moral, but he is a better member of society. No one will deny the importance of personality in its influence on positive moral qualities; but there are many people who are not influenced by personality, either human or divine. Other kinds of control, such as hygienic and legal, are necessary for such people.

(5) "A positive evil can be driven out only by a much more positive good. The lower passion can be conquered only by a higher passion." *Good and evil.*

Here, again, Dr. Cabot seems to misunderstand the aim of hygienic teaching regarding sex. It is not expected "to conquer the lower passion" by hygiene, but to help keep it under control to the end that personal and social health will be improved. The opium evil (certainly a *positive* one) is being driven out of China by military methods that are good only in their results in suppressing the drug. Likewise, hygiene of sex will be a practical good in so far as it may reduce the venereal curse. "Positive good" in Dr. Cabot's moral sense is only of limited application so far as the majority of people are concerned. In fact, the whole idea of solving the sexual problems by "consecration of the affections" makes its strong appeal only to those who have already grasped the higher view of sex and do not need sex-instruction. Other people cannot understand the phrase. We must find some more direct and practical attack on the sex problems for the masses; and I believe that this means scientific teaching which improves attitude, and hygienic teaching which protects personal and social health.

It is worth while to get these results even if we do not succeed in improving morals. That, I believe, is another and quite independent problem.

In an address published in the *Journal of the Society of Sanitary and Moral Prophylaxis*, Vol. V, No. 1, January 1914, Dr. Cabot contended that the hygienic and moral aspects of sex-education should not be associated. It is possible that the following review and criticisms may be based upon a misinterpretation; but if so, I shall not feel lonely, for at the close of the discussion, Dr. Cabot said to his audience, "it is evident that I have not succeeded in touching even the surfaces of your minds, and have not made an atom of impression in making the distinction which I desired to make."

<small>Dissociation of hygienic and moral teaching.</small>

Dr. Cabot's main points are quoted below, and my comments follow each quotation.

(1) "Sanitation can often be conveyed effectively by information, but morality cannot be conveyed by telling things."

It is certainly true that sanitation can be taught by words. That words concerning moral things have no value is a proposition which Dr. Cabot did not clearly and convincingly support.

<small>Teaching morals.</small>

(2) "People often make sanitary mistakes from ignorance. So far as you are ignorant you cannot be immoral. Morality is conditioned upon knowledge of the right and wrong in question."

Of course, one who is ignorant is unmoral and not immoral, but this does not divorce sanitary and moral problems of social disease. An ignorant and unmoral man may have unsanitary sexual habits, but enlighten him regarding venereal disease and his habits make him immoral.

<small>Immoral or unmoral.</small>

(3) "I cannot see that biology has moral value."

But it may have moral influence just as literature and history and biography may have. Of course, pure biology alone will not make people more sexually moral, but no responsible biologist has ever claimed that it will.

<small>Moral value of biology.</small>

(4) "In morals, we are dealing with the will, and if we believe that the will is guided by intelligence, we must believe that all people who *know* what is right will *do* what is right."

It does not follow that to know what is right is to do what is right. All depends upon the relative weight of opposing factors. A medical student may *know* the facts regarding venereal disease; but he also knows the fact that his sexual instincts are insistent. The fact of his passion may be more weighty than his scientific knowledge; and his will may be guided by intelligent choice based on comparison of the two opposing facts. Hence, it is illogical to contend that knowledge may not influence moral conduct and that the will is not guided by intelligence.

<small>Knowledge and will.</small>

(5) "Any good achieved in any branch of morality helps all morality. A person who learns any kind of

self control is helped toward all kinds. Anything that helps self control in one field will help in all Cultivation fields, the field of sex as well as others. of morality. Whatever makes a person more obedient to conscience in matters of truth or courage will help him in matters of chastity. We get morality not by consciously cultivating particular virtues, but by making ourselves useful men and women, by practice and by the love and imitation of our betters. Thus, morality is cultivated in hundreds of ways all at once."

This is sound, but it is in no logical way opposed to any other aspect of sex-instruction discussed in this series of lectures.

(6) "Wherever the conditions of intimacy and interest exist, — intimacy with the right person and interest in the right thing, — moral training is going on."

This is Dr. Cabot's strongest point. He be-
Influence of lieves in the moral influence of indi-
individuals. viduals. So do all leading advocates of sex-instruction or of any other form of moral education. This is in no sense opposed to any accepted proposition of sex-education.

(7) "Sanitation may increase immorality. . . . I do care more for morality than for sanitation. Where the two conflict I want morality to lead and to govern."

Right here is the basis for Dr. Cabot's repeated attacks on the sex-education movement. He believes that morality and sanitation are decidedly conflicting. His address fails to support this idea with regard to a single point concerned with the proposed sex-education. He mentioned only two points wherein there is apparent conflict, namely, prophylaxis that allows immorality while avoiding venereal disease, and prevention of conception. Neither of these is directly involved in the sex-education movement, and their immoral bearings are highly debatable. Morals rather than health.

Venereal prophylactics may increase promiscuity of some unmoral and immoral men, but if universally and scientifically used by such men, there would be little or no infection of innocent women and children. Therefore, I assert that the good that would come from the use of prophylactics by those who do not recognize moral control would be far more significant than the fact that venereal prophylactics might encourage immorality. Those who would use prophylactics would be no worse morally than they were before, but society would gain hygienically. Ethics of venereal antisepsis.

Regarding the morality of prevention of fertilization, the best of people hold opposing views. A great specialist in tuberculosis who entered the discussion of Dr. Cabot's paper convinced most of his hearers that hygienic prevention of fertilization of tubercular women is a very moral act for a physician to advise. The real question of morality involved in the problem of contraconception is not whether it is immoral that sperm-cells should be prevented from Ethics of contraconception.

swimming on towards an egg-cell, but whether there is morality in a sexual union that has its meaning only in affection and is not definitely intended for propagation. It is obviously a complicated problem of hygiene, psychology, ethics, æsthetics, religious beliefs, social traditions, and personal prejudice; and it is absurd to allow it to become entangled in the general propositions of sex-education. As I have often said in this series of lectures, the larger sex-education aims at making the best possible adjustments of sex and life. If the æsthetic demands of affection are in real conflict with the animal function of propagation, then a pragmatically ethical solution is found in intelligent control of the original function. Ideally, the animal function of propagation should be associated with the possibilities of affection that have developed in the highest human life; but there are numerous cases in which there must be dissociation of the functions of affection and propagation, or the alternative is sexual asceticism. Which is moral? This is a question concerning which the individual must weigh his personal views and decide. Only the bigoted victims of arrogance will see immorality in the one who disagrees with him on this question. I insist, then, that even if advanced sex-education for adults should some day come to involve the problem of contraconception, there will be no conflict between hygienic knowledge and ethics, if the teaching leads to more perfect adjustment of sex and life.

Probably the great majority of workers in the sex-education movement do not in the least agree with Dr. Cabot's attempts to dissociate hygienic and moral problems. A far more helpful view is that expressed by Dr. Henry Neumann, leader of the Brooklyn Ethical Culture Society: *Dr. Neumann's view.*

"Problems of hygiene, whether of sex, or nutrition, or temperance and the like, are no less moral problems. They are problems of habit; and habits are impossible without strong incentives to start them and keep them going. . . . Ethical instruction is often misunderstood to be barren preaching. It is nothing of the sort. It consists in clarifying views of life. It begins with the fact that there are certain tendencies in our nature which may work ill or good. Then it tries to show to what these lead. It uses what is best in us to make over what is worst. That is why problems of sex-hygiene should be regarded as at bottom problems of sex-morality."

§ 47. *The Arrogance of the Advocates of Sex-education*

In an article in the *Educational Review*, February, 1914, Superintendent Maxwell, of New York City, writes concerning what he calls "the teaching of child hygiene" as follows:

"There are those to-day who claim that sexual information and problems should be thrust upon the attention of boys and girls by the teachers in the public schools, that this teaching is necessary for the protection of virtue and the prevention of disease, and that, if anyone hesitates to encourage the spread of such *Dr. Maxwell's criticisms.*

literature and the teaching of such knowledge, he is an arrant and presumptuous blockhead. The arrogance of the extreme advocates of child hygiene blinds them to certain all-important truths. The first is that our teachers are not prepared, and, in too many cases, are not the most suitable persons to teach the subject. The second is that to bring the adolescent mind face to face with sexual matters engenders the habit of dwelling upon the sexual passion, and in that may lie spiritual havoc and physical ruin. A premature interest in the sexual passion debases the mind and unsettles the will. The third is that parents have no right to ask the teacher to do the work that is peculiarly theirs.

"And yet some good may emerge from this discussion. Parents may be incited to do their duty in placing sex information before their children whenever conditions demand such knowledge. And principals and teachers, particularly principals, whenever they have the acuteness to detect the tendency to wrong-doing, will no longer hesitate to utter the word of warning in season. As for the extravagant claims made for the teaching of sex-hygiene, I have too much faith in the good sense of the American people to believe that it will ever be generally and regularly taught in American schools. Surely, we have learned something since the law compelled us to teach the untruths regarding the effects of stimulants and narcotics that were published in the early school manuals of physiology and hygiene."

I comment as follows: (1) Dr. Maxwell refers only to the "extreme advocates." They did exist in abundance a few years ago, but are already rare in the group of well-known educators. (2) Most teachers are not prepared and never can be prepared to teach the human aspect of sex problems, especially the hygienic in the strict sense. (3) Conservative sex-instruction such as was advocated by the advisers of the American Federation for Sex-hygiene (see "Report" by Morrow and others, 1913) aims to guard against "premature interest in the sexual passion." (4) While I sympathize with Dr. Maxwell's view that teaching the elementary hygiene of sex is the parent's duty, I am forced to recognize the futility of advocating that all or even a respectable minority of parents should undertake their duty (see § 4). The truth is that most of them will not, and cannot if they will, try to do so. (5) Dr. Maxwell's idea that sex-hygiene should be taught only when an astute principal or parent "detects wrong-doing" is, to say the least, an educational theory that will astonish one who knows even the elementary facts regarding the secrecy of the sexual life of young people in general. Will he next be logically consistent and advocate that all moral education should be given only after children show signs of wrong-doing? (6) Sex-hygiene, as Dr. Maxwell understands it to be concerned directly and solely with human sexual problems, will never be taught in American schools controlled by people of good sense; but sex-instruction from the larger viewpoint is taught in some of the best of Dr. Maxwell's high schools. (7) All advocates of sex-instruction who have a national reputation for educational sanity

Reply to Dr. Maxwell.

agree that legislation is most undesirable. (8) It is obvious that like so many others who have become confused regarding the sex-education movement, Dr. Maxwell has been impressed chiefly by the pioneer work that emphasized only hygienic teaching regarding sex.

§ 48. *Lubricity in Education*

Ex-President Taft has expressed his views against the sex-education movement. The newspapers quote as follows from an address delivered in Philadelphia in 1914:

"There is another danger in our educational influences and environment. I refer to the spread of lubricity in literature, on the stage and indirectly in education, under the plea that vice may be avoided by teaching the awful consequences. By dwelling on its details and explaining its penalties, sexual subjects are obtruded into discussion between the sexes, lectures are delivered on them, textbooks are written, and former restraints of modesty are abandoned.

"The pursuit of education in sex-hygiene is full of danger if carried on in general public schools. The sharp, pointed and summary advice of mothers to daughters, of fathers to sons, of a medical professor to students in a college upon such a subject is, of course, wise, but any benefit that may be derived from frightening students by dwelling upon the details of the dreadful punishment of vice is too often offset by awakening a curiosity and interest that might not be developed so early and is likely to set the thoughts of those whose benefit is at stake in a direction that will

Mr. Taft's alarm.

neither elevate their conversations with their fellows nor make more clean their mental habit.

"I deny that the so-called prudishness and the avoidance of nasty subjects in the last generation has ever blinded any substantial number of girls or boys to the wickedness of vice or made them easier victims of temptations."

The above requires little comment, for its misunderstandings are obvious to one who has followed the sex-education movement. Clearly Mr. Taft has been impressed by the social-hygiene side of the problems and does not realize the existence of a larger outlook for sex-education. Like so many other writers who seem to know little concerning the sexual life of children, especially of boys, Mr. Taft fears "the awakening of curiosity and interest"! This, of course, depends upon the facts taught and the age of the learner, but it hardly applies to children in or near adolescence who are taught along the lines suggested by the committee of the American Federation for Sex-Hygiene (1913). The last paragraph quoted from Mr. Taft will be denied completely by all who are familiar with the problems of adolescent education. To say the least, it is unfortunate that a man prominent in law and statesmanship should have lent the weight of his name to such superficial conclusions that are so obviously based on exceedingly limited information regarding both the established facts of sex and the most approved methods of sex-instruction.

Evident misunderstanding.

§ 49. *Conclusions from the Criticisms of Sex-education*

I have selected for discussion the criticisms of several of the most prominent people who have expressed opposition to the sex-education movement. I think that all the important lines of arguments against the movement are represented in the extracts that I have quoted. We have seen that all of the criticisms have decidedly vulnerable points. Most of them refer to the discarded sex-hygiene of ten years ago; but some of them prove that the authors are quite ignorant of the sex problems that must be faced by numerous young people.

With the hope of locating the weaknesses of sex-education, I have for years examined carefully every criticism published, and it seems to me thoroughly scientific to conclude that all the important criticisms have not harmed the essentials of the sex-education movement; but, on the contrary, have been helpful in forcing reconstruction. In fact, the present-day conception of the larger sex-education must be credited to the severe critics more than to the friends of the original narrow movement for reducing venereal disease by hygienic instruction.

Criticisms important.

XI

The Past and the Future of the Sex-Education Movement

§ 50. *The American Movement*

In America the movement for sex-education began with the organization of the American Society of Sanitary and Moral Prophylaxis on February 9, 1905, under the leadership of Dr. Prince A. Morrow. It is true that before this time there were various local and sporadic attempts at instruction concerning sexual processes, but such teaching was chiefly personal and there was no concerted movement looking towards making sex-instruction an integral part of general education. In 1892, thirteen years before the organization of the Society of Sanitary and Moral Prophylaxis, a group of members of the National Education Association considered briefly the importance of instructing young people. However, this meeting was of ephemeral significance and had no genetic relation to the present-day movement. Other early interest in sex-instruction is indicated in Professor Earl Barnes's bibliography which was published in his "Studies in Education," Vol. I, p. 301, 1897.

[margin: Dr. Morrow leader in America.]

The educational activities, especially the publications of the American Society of Sanitary and Moral Prophylaxis, soon attracted the serious attention of numerous physicians, ministers, and educators in various parts of the United States; and about twenty other societies for study and improvement of the sex problems were organized within a few years after the original society.

The sex-education movement both in Europe and America had its origin as an attempt to check the spread of the venereal or social diseases. The idea that education should work for sexual morality for its own sake and not simply for protection against venereal diseases has only recently begun to appear in the literature of sex-education, and so far it seems to have made only a limited impression on many of those who have been active in the prophylactic campaign against social disease. In fact, the tardy recognition of the moral aim of sex-education makes it seem probable that very little interest would have been aroused in the movement if it had been organized on purely ethical grounds and without any reference to the sanitary problems of social diseases. To one who looks at sexual morality as a question of right conduct which brings its own rewards, it is a shock to find so many thinking people who accept calmly the traditional views of the relation of the sexes and seem to take no interest in the immorality of men except as it is likely to lead to venereal disease or to illegitimacy which

Original aim for sanitary ends.

demands forced marriage or monetary payments. The truth is that the civilized world at large is very far from a working code of sexual morals which will be practiced because of promised rewards rather than because of probable punishments. It is natural, then, that the sex-education movement should have started with a proclamation of physical punishments for immorality rather than an offer of ethical and psychical rewards for morality.

However, the fact that sex-education, under the name of "sex-hygiene," was at first a sanitary propagandism need not interfere with the larger development of sex-education. It now seems probable that before many years pass we shall learn how to make a satisfactory combination of both the sanitary and moral sides of sex-education, and so it is best that the educational movement started on the foundation of the undisputed facts of sanitary science which have made a powerful impression on the people who do and who do not recognize a code of sexual morals. *Both sanitary and moral.*

The deep interest of the medical profession is directly responsible for the close association between the beginning of the sex-education movement and the diseases of immorality. At the organization meeting of the American Society of Sanitary and Moral Prophylaxis, Dr. Prince Morrow in the opening paragraph of his address said: "We have met for the purpose of discussing the wisdom and the expediency of forming a society of sanitary and moral prophylaxis. The object *Medical interest.*

is to organize a social defense against a class of diseases which are most injurious to the highest interests of human society." Thus, the American Society of Sanitary and Moral Prophylaxis started as an avowed enemy of the social diseases and so it has continued to the present. The very name of its official journal, *Social Diseases*,[1] indicated the central idea of the Society. Likewise, most of the local American societies for sex-hygiene have names including such phrases as "social hygiene," "prevention of social diseases," "sanitary prophylaxis"; and only one, the Massachusetts Society for Sex Education, has a name which does not directly suggest the medical problems of sex.

In Europe, the sex-instruction movement has been concerned chiefly with spreading information concerning the social diseases. In 1902 an international congress for consideration of the venereal diseases was held in Brussels, and this congress recommended that in all countries there should be organized sanitary, social, moral, and legal societies for the prophylaxis of these diseases. As a result of this recommendation, prophylactic societies were formed in France, Germany, Italy, Holland, the United States, and other countries. Of these, the German society for the prevention of venereal disease became the strongest, with over five thousand members and twenty branch societies.

In Europe.

[1] The name was changed in 1913 to *Journal of the Society of Sanitary and Moral Prophylaxis*.

The fact that the American Society of Sanitary and Moral Prophylaxis was organized by a group of people in New York City tended from the beginning to make it a local society. **National societies.** While for several years it took the lead in sex-hygiene and enrolled members residing in many parts of the United States, it was never a national organization. In recent years the word "American" has been omitted from its name, and its work has been limited to New York City and vicinity.[1] Many independent state and city societies were organized within a few years after the original sex-hygiene society in New York. This multiplication of societies called attention to the need of a national organization, and in 1910 the various societies were affiliated in the American Federation for Sex-Hygiene. Dr. Morrow was the leading spirit in the Federation until his death. In 1913, the Federation and the American Vigilance Association (a society especially concerned with the social evil) were united in the American Social Hygiene Association. Its offices are at 105 West 40th Street, New York City.

§ 51. *Important Steps in the Sex-education Movement in America*

May 23, 1904. Dr. Prince Morrow's plea for the organization of a society of sanitary and moral prophylaxis, read before the Medical Society of the County of New York.

---

[1] While this book was in press, the name was changed to New York Social Hygiene Society.

February 9, 1905. Organization meeting of the American Society of Sanitary and Moral Prophylaxis, in New York.

March, 1906. Pennsylvania Society for the Prevention of Social Diseases organized.

October, 1906. Chicago Society of Social Hygiene organized.

December, 1907. Portland (Ore.) Social Hygiene Society organized.

October, 1908. Spokane Society of Social and Moral Prophylaxis organized.

June, 1910. American Federation for Sex-Hygiene organized.

1911. Oregon Social Hygiene Society organized.

July 20, 1912. Resolution of the National Education Association favoring training of teachers with the view, ultimately, of sex-instruction in schools.

September 23-28, 1912. Meeting of subsection on sex-hygiene, Fifteenth International Congress on Hygiene and Demography. Washington, D.C.

February, 1912. Organization of American Vigilance Association.

October, 1913. Merging of the American Federation for Sex-Hygiene and the American Vigilance Association into the new American Social Hygiene Association.

1913. Organization of Pacific Coast Federation for Sex-Hygiene, changed to Pacific Coast Social Hygiene Association in June, 1914.

July, 1914. The National Education Association, at Minneapolis, adopted the following resolutions in line with the latest principles of the Society of Sanitary and Moral Prophylaxis and the American Social Hygiene Association:

"The Association, re-affirming its belief in the constructive value of education in sex-hygiene, directs attention to the grave dangers, ethical and social, arising out of a sex consciousness stimulated by undue emphasis upon sex problems and relations. The situation is so serious as to render neglect hazardous. The Association urges upon all parents the obvious duty of parental care and instruction in such matters and directs attention to the mistake of leaving such problems exclusively to the school. The Association believes that sex-hygiene should be approached in the public schools conservatively under the direction of persons qualified by scientific training and teaching experience in order to assure a safe moral point of view. The Association, therefore, recommends that institutions preparing teachers give attention to such subjects as would qualify for instruction in the general field of morals as well as in the particular field of sex-hygiene."

§ 52. *The Future of the Larger Sex-education*

I hear many questions as to the probable future of sex-education. I am asked: "Is it moribund?" "Is it a disappearing fad?" "Has not the high tide of interest passed?" No doubt such questions are inspired by the oft-repeated statement that public interest in sexual questions has waned decidedly in the last few years. This is true, and it is a most fortunate indication of approaching sanity. The public interest in the last decade has been most deplorable, because it has centered in the abnormal and sensational aspects of sex. Authors have vied with each other in presenting the most lurid cases of social diseases, white slavery, sexual perversions, and every other available aspect of sexual degeneracy. Of course, the reading public was bound to grow tired of this, just as it wearies

Public has lost interest in sensationalism.

of a horrible murder trial or of a sensational divorce case. It is certainly true that there is a marked decline of general interest in sexual abnormality and sensationalism; but that does not mean that the sex-education movement is moribund.

The wave of sensational revelation has passed; but the intelligent public is no longer ignorant of the nature and causes of the great problems of sex, and is well aware that young people need definite guidance for facing the facts of life. It is unthinkable that intelligent parents who are now well informed concerning sex will ever again stand for the old policy of mystery and silence. It is, therefore, impossible to believe that there is any danger of sex-education disappearing. Of course, we have not reached a permanent system of sex-education. There certainly will be vast changes in our approved subject matter and methods of teaching; but the main idea of the sex-education movement is gaining support every day.

Sex-education permanent.

There is another reason why sex-education will be permanent. In addition to the great need of educational help with information and influence which will mold the individual life with regard to the problems of sex, it must be evident to all that even the legislative, sanitary, social administrative, religious, ethical, and other attacks upon the problems depend upon knowledge and attitude, at least of the leaders. Look at the problems of sex outlined in the earlier lectures from whatever angle we will, and it appears

Sex-education fundamental.

that, in the final analysis, education offers the only key to a possible solution. Therefore, I assert that sex-education — the larger sex-education — is an absolutely fundamental factor in every phase of the social-hygiene and sex-ethical movement.

In closing the last lecture of this series, let me state my confession of faith in sex-education: It is certainly only *one of several* possible lines of attack on the alarming sex problems of our time; but it offers the most hopeful outlook towards improved sexual morals and health, both physical and psychical. However, we shall gain nothing of permanent value by extravagant claims or hopes as to the ultimate effect of sex-education. We must expect incomplete results. It will not entirely solve the sex problems for all individuals who receive instruction; but it will solve all of the problems of many individuals and help many others. It will not eradicate the social evil and its characteristic diseases, but it will protect many young people and so reduce the sum total of awful consequences. It will not prevent all divorces and matrimonial disharmonies, but already the biological teaching is helping and some day the social-ethical problems will be understood and then most intelligent men and women will understand the fundamental principles for permanent and harmonious monogamic marriage. Finally, sex-education will not enforce universal sexual morality in conformity with our accepted code, but it will help many individuals through decisive battles with sex-instincts.

<small>Ultimate effect of sex-education.</small>

Such are some of the lines along which extreme claims and hopes for sex-education have been and are still being made. There is some truth in each; in fact, there is more than enough to justify the present movement for sex-education. To all those who see nothing in the movement because it will not solve all the sex problems which have created a demand for special instruction, we may reply by simply pointing to the fact that general education makes some better and more efficient citizens, but many times it fails to give desirable results. We believe in general education because it aims to offer all individuals help in preparation for more efficient life, although it succeeds only in part. Likewise, we should stand for the instruction of all young people in matters concerning sex because it is certain that such knowledge will function completely in many lives and will work appreciable good in many others.

Sex-education and general education.

I cannot believe that sex-education is one of the long line of modern educational fads which quickly pass their day, for no other phase of education so closely touches life. History and geography and even a large part of the "three Rs" may be of little use in the lives of numerous people, but sex-education deals with problems which the normal human life cannot possibly avoid and which each individual must be prepared to solve for himself. Therefore, we may confidently assert that instruction concerning the most important aspects of sex processes and relationships will

A permanent and essential part of education.

soon be recognized as an absolutely necessary part of a rational and efficient scheme for the education of young people.

The larger sex-education is sure to have a permanent place in the never-ending work of preparing coming generations for the highest development of life's possibilities. Each succeeding generation of young people must be prepared by educational processes to face intelligently and bravely the problems of sex that are sure to come into every normal life. Of course, sex-education at its best development can do no more than give the individual a basis for intelligent choice between good and evil; but here, as in all other upward movements of human life, the decision must depend upon a clear and positive recognition of the advantages of the good as contrasted with the evil. Hence, the one essential task of sex-education in its broadest outlook is to guide natural human beings to recognition and choice of the best in the sexual sphere of life. And in so far as each coming generation of individuals may be thus guided by the larger sex-education, the problems of sex will be pragmatically solved, for the social aggregate of human life will become better, happier, nobler, truer, more in harmony with the highest ideals of life, more like our vision of perfected humanity.

The never-ending problem of good and evil.

XII

Some Books for Sex–Education

I have decided to publish only the names of selected books which seem to me to be the best for teachers, parents, and young people. In making the selection, I have considered several hundred books which bear on the sex problems in an educational way, and have decided to reject the majority of them. While there might be some value in a long list with critical notes on books that I cannot recommend, it would be a worse than thankless task to compile such an annotated bibliography; for the compiler would surely add to his collection of enemies many authors whose books deserve severe criticism. The sudden and sensational publicity concerning matters of sex and the possibility of commercial exploitation has produced an avalanche of sex books, some good, many bad, and the majority ordinary. Evidently, most of the authors, including numerous physicians, have written to order and without special preparation.

The books of the following lists are not all deserving of unqualified recommendation. In fact, some of them are included because they are the least objectionable of their much-needed kind, and others because they have some good grains that the reader will find worth picking from a mass of non-nutritious but, fortunately, non-poisonous chaff.

I have not included many books which I recognize as important for readers thoroughly trained in science, but which are dangerous for the average reader of literature on sex.

It is possible that I may have overlooked some very good books that I have not intended to ignore; and I shall be glad to have my attention called to books which deserve recognition.

Special bibliographies have been published in Wile's "Sex-Education," March's "Towards Racial Health," Geddes and Thomson's "Sex," and Foster's "Social Emergency."

Publishers. — In most cases the first part of the names of well-known publishers has been given. Unless otherwise mentioned, they have offices in New York City. In addition, the following abbreviations have been used:

A.M.A. = American Medical Association, Chicago.

A.S.H.A. = American Social Hygiene Association, 105 West 40th St., New York City.

S.S.M.P. = Society of Sanitary and Moral Prophylaxis, 105 West 40th Street, New York City.

Association Press = press of the National Board of the Y.M.C.A., New York City.

For Educators and Parents

Addams, Jane. "A New Conscience and an Ancient Evil."
    Macmillan. $1.00. (Contains all the average reader needs to know concerning prostitution.)

Bok, Edward, Editor. "Books of Self-Knowledge for Young People and Parents." Revell. $.25 each.

Bigelow, M. A. "Relation of Biology to Sex-Instruction in Schools and Colleges." Journal of Social Diseases, II, 4, October, 1911.

Cabot, Richard C. "The Christian Approach to Social Morality." National Y.W.C.A., New York. $.50.

Cabot, Richard C. "What Men Live By." Houghton Mifflin. $1.50. (A book that has helped many people.)

Cabot, R. C. "Consecration of the Affections." Proceedings of Fifth Cong. Amer. School Hygiene Assoc., III, 1911, p. 114. Also in Amer. Phy. Ed. Rev., XVI, 1911, pp. 247–253. (See "Criticisms of Sex-Education" in § 46 of this book.)

Cocks, Orrin G. "The Social Evil and Methods of Treatment." Association Press. $.25.

Creighton, Louise. "The Social Disease and How to Fight It." Longmans. $.35. (A splendid essay on social impurity from a modern woman's viewpoint. Constructive and optimistic.)

Eliot, C. W. "Public Opinion and Sex-Hygiene." A.S.H.A. $.05.

Eliot, C. W. "School Instruction in Sex Hygiene." Proceedings of Fifth Cong. Amer. School Hygiene Assoc., 1911.

Ellis, Havelock. "The Task of Social Hygiene." Houghton. $2.50. (Certain chapters concern sex-education.)

Galloway, T. W. "Biology of Sex." Heath. $.75.

Geddes, Patrick, and Thomson, J. Arthur. "Sex." Holt. $.50. (Excellent.)

Geddes and Thomson. "The Problems of Sex." Moffat. $.50.

Foster, W. T. "The Social Emergency." Houghton. $1.35. (Twelve excellent essays by President Foster, Reed College, and nine others, on social hygiene and education.)

Hall, G. Stanley. "Adolescence." Appleton. 2 vols. $7.50.

HALL, G. S. "Youth: Its Education, Regimen and Hygiene." Appleton. $1.50.

HALL, G. S. "Needs and Methods of Educating Young People in Hygiene of Sex." Pedagogical Seminary, XV, March, 1908.

HALL, G. S. "Teaching of Sex in Schools and Colleges." Journal of Social Diseases, II, 4, October, 1911.

HALL, WINFIELD S. "Sex Training in the Home." Richardson, Chicago. $1.10.

HENDERSON, CHAS. R. "Education with Reference to Sex." University of Chicago Press. Part I, 78 cts.; II, 80 cts. (Part I demonstrates need of sex-education; II, the educational problems.)

HERTER, C. A. "Biological Aspects of Human Problems." Macmillan. $1.50. (Sexual instincts, pp. 182–252; sex-education, 306–316.)

HIME, MAURICE C. "Schoolboys' Special Immorality." Churchill, London. $.40. (For masters of boarding schools.)

HODGE, C. F. "Social Hygiene in Public Schools." School Science and Mathematics, April, 1911.

HOWARD, W. L. "Start Your Child Right." Revell. $.75. (Readable, sensible, helpful to parents.)

LOWRY, EDITH B. "False Modesty: That Protects Vice by Ignorance." Forbes. $.50. (Arguments for sex-instruction in home and school.)

LOWRY, E. B. "Teaching Sex-Hygiene in the Public Schools." Forbes. $.50. (Useful for parents and teachers.)

LYTTLETON, E. "Training the Young in the Laws of Sex." Longmans, Green. $1.00. (Heartily approved by many educators.)

MARCH, NORAH H. "Towards Racial Health." Routledge, London. $1.00. (Very helpful book for parents and teachers.)

MORLEY, MARGARET W. "Renewal of Life." McClurg. $1.10. (Nature-study basis for teaching children.)

MORROW, BALLIET, and BIGELOW. "Report of Special Committee on Matters and Methods of Sex-Education." A.S.H.A. $.05.
MORROW, PRINCE A. "Teaching of Sex-Hygiene." A.S.H.A. $.03. (A splendid address.)
MORROW, P. A. "The Boy Problem." S.S.M.P. $.05. (Helpful to parents.)
MORROW, P. A. "The Sex Problem." S.S.M.P. $.03. (A fair statement of the double morality problem.)
PARKINSON, WILLIAM D. "Sex and Education." Educational Review, January, 1911. (Stands for ethical and æsthetic teaching primarily.)
SCHARLIEB and SIBLY. "Youth and Sex." Dodge. $.25.
SELIGMAN, E. R. A. "The Social Evil." Putnam. $1.50. (A good survey of the evil, based on the work of the Committee of Fourteen in New York.)
WILE, IRA S. "Sex Education." Duffield. $1.00. (A very useful book for parents.)
WOOD-ALLEN, MARY. "Teaching Truth." Crist Co. $.50. Suggestions for mothers' talks to young children.)
"Social Hygiene." A quarterly journal of the A.S.H.A. $2.00 per year, free to members.

FOR GIRLS

ADDAMS, JANE. "Spirit of Youth and the City Streets." Macmillan. $1.25.
CHAPMAN, ROSE WOODALLEN. "How Shall I Tell My Child?" Revell. $.25.
DODGE, GRACE H. "A Bundle of Letters to Busy Girls." Funk. $.50.
HALL, JEANNETTE W. "Life's Story." Steadwell, La Crosse, Wis. $.25. (Biological facts for girls of 10 to 16.)
HALL, W. S. "Life Problems: A Story for Girls." A.M.A. $.10. (A good pamphlet for girls of 12 to 18 years.)

HALL, W. S. "The Doctor's Daughter: Studies about Life." A.M.A. $.10. (On nature-study basis, for girls under 12 years.)

HOOD, MARY G. "For Girls and the Mothers of Girls." Bobbs-Merrill. $1.00.

HOWARD, W. L. "Confidential Chats with Girls." Clode. $1.00.

SMITH, NELLIE M. "The Three Gifts of Life." Dodd, Mead. $.50. (A girl's responsibility. For girls 15 to 18, who have no more than grammar-school education. In general, sentimental and unscientific; but Chapter IV, "Gift of Choice," is excellent.)

TORELLE, ELLEN. "Plant and Animal Children: How they Grow." Heath. $1.00. (Useful as a nature-study reader concerning reproduction of animals and plants.)

WOOD-ALLEN, MARY. "Almost a Woman." Crist Co. $.50. (A story for girls of 12 years.)

WOOD-ALLEN, MARY. "What a Young Girl Should Know." Vir Co., Philadelphia. $1.00. (For girls under 12 or 14.)

FOR BOYS

HALL, W. S. "John's Vacation." A.M.A. $.10. (On nature-study basis, for pre-adolescent boys.)

HALL, W. S. "Chums." A.M.A. $.10. (For adolescent boys.)

HALL, W. S. "Developing into Manhood." Association Press. $.25. (Biological basis, for boys of 15 to 18 years.)

HALL, W. S. "Life's Beginnings." Association Press. $.25.

HALL, W. S. "Youth." Association Press. $.25. (For boys 10 to 12.)

HOWARD, W. L. "Confidential Chats with Boys." Clode. $1.00.

JENKS, J. W. "Life Questions of School Boys." Association Press. $.25.

JEWETT. "The Next Generation." Ginn. $.75. (Elementary eugenics.)
TORELLE, ELLEN. "Plant and Animal Children." (See under books for girls.)
TREWBY, ARTHUR. "Healthy Boyhood." Longmans. $.40.
WOOD-ALLEN, MARY. "Almost a Man." Crist Co. $.50. (Similar to "Almost a Woman." For pre-adolescent boys.)

FOR WOMEN

DRAKE, E. F. A. "What a Young Wife Ought to Know." Vir Co., Philadelphia. $1.00.
GALBRAITH, ANNA. "Four Epochs of a Woman's Life." Saunders, Philadelphia. $1.50. (Medical in style. Certain sections relating to heredity are not satisfactory.)
HALL, W. S. "Sexual Knowledge." Intern. Bible House, Philadelphia. $1.00.
KEY, ELLEN. "Morality of Woman and other Essays." Seymour, Chicago. $1.00. (Ideal morality as a basis for marriage. Good introduction to author's "Love and Marriage.")
LOWRY, E. B. "Herself." Forbes. $1.10. (In general, accurate. Medical style.)
MARTIN, H. N. "Human Body — Advanced Course." Holt. $2.50. (Last chapter, on reproduction, excellent.)
RUMMEL, LUELLA Z. "Womanhood and Its Development." Burton Co., Kansas City. $1.50. (One of the best books for mature women. Poorly printed.)
SCHREINER, OLIVE. "Woman and Labor." Stokes. $1.25. (Important for the feminist movement.)
WEST, MRS. MAX. "Prenatal Care." Bulletin of Children's Bureau, U. S. Dept. of Labor. (A very practical pamphlet.)
WOOD-ALLEN, MARY. "What a Young Woman Should Know." Vir Co., Philadelphia. $1.00. (The best-known book, preferred by the majority of mothers.)

For Men

Exner, M. J. "Problems and Principles of Sex-Education." Association Press. $.10. (Study of college men, and an essay on principles.)

Exner, M. J. "The Physician's Answer." Association Press. $.15. (Summary of opinions of numerous physicians concerning the problems of young men.)

Exner, M. J. "The Rational Sex Life for Men." Association Press. $.15. (Good, and helpful to many young men.)

Hall, W. S. "From Youth into Manhood." Association Press. $.50. (Highly approved and widely used.)

Hall, W. S. "Instead of Wild Oats." Revell. $.25. (Bok Series, Biological and Sociological basis.)

Hall, W. S. "Reproduction and Sexual Hygiene." Wynnewood, Chicago. $.90. (Very useful book, but criticized by many who disagree with the hygienic part.)

Hall, W. S. "Sexual Knowledge." Intern. Bible House. Philadelphia. $1.00. (Useful for both men and women. Includes the best of the above book.)

Howard, William Lee. "Plain Facts on Sex Hygiene." Clode. $1.00. (Sensational and exaggerated statements concerning social diseases; language unnecessarily offensive in places; but discussion of "continence" is good.)

Howell and Keyes. "The Sexual Necessity." S.S.M.P. $.03.

Lowry, E. B., and Lambert, R. J. "Himself: Talks with Men concerning Themselves." Forbes. $1.00. (Accurate in facts; not well arranged; not "the best book," as the publishers claim.)

Lydston, G. Frank. "Sex Hygiene for the Male." Riverton, Chicago. $2.25. (Readable, fairly reliable, but not worth the price.)

Martin, H. N. "Human Body — Advanced Course." Holt. $2.50. (Last chapter, especially in 1910 edition.)

Moore, H. H. "Keeping in Condition." Macmillan. $1.00. (A physical training book.)

MORROW, PRINCE A. "Health and Hygiene of Sex." S.S.M.P. $.05. (The best-known pamphlet for college men.)

SPEER, ROBERT E. "A Young Man's Questions." Revell. $.80.

SPERRY, LYMAN B. "Confidential Talks with Young Men." Revell. $.75.

STALL, SYLVANUS. "What a Young Husband Ought to Know." Vir Co., Philadelphia. $1.00. (This and the next are useful to men who prefer a religious approach to sexual information.)

STALL, SYLVANUS. "What a Young Man Ought to Know." Vir Co., Philadelphia. $1.00.

WILSON, ROBERT N. "American Boy and the Social Evil." Winston. $1.00.

FOR THE MARRIED

COCKS, ORRIN G. "Engagement and Marriage." Association Press. $.25. (Talks to young men, but young women should be interested.)

COWAN, JOHN. "Science of a New Life." 1869. $3.00. (Obsolete, unreliable, unscientific; but widely sold by magazine advertising.)

DAVIDSON, HUGH S. "Marriage and Motherhood." Dodge. $.25.

DAVIS, E. P. "Mother and Child." Lippincott. $1.50.

FOERSTER, F. W. "Marriage and the Sex Problem." Stokes. $1.35. (An important book.)

HOLT, L. E. "Care and Feeding of Children." Appleton. $.75. (The well-known nursery guide by the famous pediatrician.)

HOWARD, W. L. "Facts for the Married." Clode. $1.00. (Good, from a physician's standpoint.)

JORDAN, W. J. "Little Problems of Married Life." Revell. $1.00. (Essays which touch many problems of home life.)

KEY, ELLEN. "Love and Marriage." Putnam. $1.50. (The greatest work of this famous Swedish author.)

SALEEBY, C. W. "Parenthood and Race Culture." Moffat, Yard. $2.50. (Popular eugenics.)
SPERRY, LYMAN B. "Confidential Talks with Husband and Wife." Revell. $1.00.
WOOD-ALLEN, MARY. "Ideal Married Life." Revell. $1.25. (Best book by this well-known physician and author.)

HEREDITY AND EUGENICS

CASTLE, W. E. "Heredity in Relation to Evolution and Animal Breeding." Appleton. $1.50.
CONKLIN, F. G. "Heredity and Environment in the Development of Men." Princeton University Press. $2.00.
DAVENPORT, C. B. "Heredity in Relation to Eugenics." Holt. $2.00.
DAWSON, G. E. "Right of the Child to be Well Born." Funk. $.75.
DONCASTER, L. "Heredity in the Light of Recent Research." Putnam. $.40.
GEDDES, P., and THOMSON, J. A. "Evolution." Holt. $.50.
GUYER, M. F. "Being Well Born." Bobbs-Merrill. $1.00.
KELLICOTT, W. E. "The Social Direction of Human Evolution." Appleton. $1.50.
PUNNETT, R. C. "Mendelism." Macmillan. $.50.
SALEEBY, C. W. "Parenthood and Race Culture." Moffat, Yard. $2.50.
THOMSON, J. A. "Heredity." Putnam. $3.50.
WALTER, H. E. "Genetics." Macmillan. $1.50.

INDEX

Abnormality, in literature, 129 ff.
Adolescence, and sex-instruction, 146 ff.
Adults, and special sex-instruction, 26.
Æsthetics of sex, 4, 74, 197.
Affection, 163; "consecration of," 210; in marriage, 189.
Aims, of sex-education, 92, 94; of sex-education societies, 228.
Animals, and human sexuality, 72.
Arguments, for sex-instruction, 28 ff.
Asceticism, 69.
Athletics, and sex, 141.
Attitude, towards sex, 26, 67 ff.; and morals, 75.

Bibliography, 238 ff.
Biology, 56, 65; and ethics, 102 ff.; and sex-instruction, 147; moral value, 217.
Books, as teachers, 121 ff., 241 ff.; see also literature.
Boys, influence on, 158; special instruction, 148–150.

Cabot, R. C., 63, 210 ff.
Childhood, 25.
Children, ignorant of sex, 204.
Circumcision, 139.
Coeducation, in sex-instruction, 109; and sex adjustment, 80.
Continence, 160 ff., 176 ff.; of women, 190 ff.
Contraception, and ethics, 219.
Control, of sex instincts, 18.

Criticisms, of sex-education, 203 ff.; conclusions regarding, 226.
Curiosity, denied by Repplier and Taft, q.v.

Dancing, 169 ff., 200.
Diseases, social or venereal, 37 ff.
Dress, of women, 174 ff., 200.

Education, as a solution, 19, 88; coeducation, 80; sex-differentiated, 82.
Eliot, C. W., 71.
Emissions, 149.
Ethics, and biology, 102; and sex-hygiene, 61 ff.; of sex, 4.
Eugenics, 86 ff.; aim of, 105; and ethics, 103.
Europe, and sex problems, 59 ff.; morality in, 59; sex-hygiene in, 230.
Evolution, and vulgarity, 75.

Fiction, and sex tragedies, 127.
Foerster, 70.
Frankness, 206.
Friendships, of children, 136.
Fulton, J. S., 40.
Future, of sex-education, 234–237.

Genetics, 87.
Girls, special instruction, 151; unprotected, 191.
Gonorrhea, see Diseases.
Good, and evil, 215.

Hamilton, Cosmo, 208.
Hartley, C. Gasquoine, 82 ff.

249

Heredity, 87; and sex-education, 104.
History, of sex-education, 227 ff.
Homes, and sex-instruction, 21.
Hunger, two kinds, 73.
Hygiene, and ethics, 210 ff.; of sex, 1-4, 25.

Ideals, of manhood, 185; of womanhood, 157; of love and marriage, 159, 187.
Ignorance, 45, 50, 54; of children, 12-14.
Illegitimacy, 52 ff., 59.
Immorality, 38; danger in teaching, 67.
Instincts, sexual, 16-18.
Intellectualism, and sex, 83.

Kallikak family, 103.
Key, Ellen, 64, 79.
Knowledge, and will, 217.

Lectures, on sex-hygiene, 100.
Legislation, and social diseases, 47.
Literature, general list, 241 ff.; for parents, 33; on marriage, 79; on diseases, 39; on sex, 11; on social evil, 52; general and sex, 124 ff.; general references, 238 ff.; for young men, 161, 183; for young women, 201; radical sex, 193.

Marriage, 159, 187; a sex problem, 71 ff.
Masturbation, 137 ff.
Maxwell, W. H., 221.
Men, as leaders in love, 188; instruction for, 156 ff.
Misunderstanding, of sex, 5.
Monogamy, 59.
Morality, 58 ff.; double standard, 42.
Morrow, P. A., 37, 70; leader, 227.

Mothercraft, 155.
Mothers, and boys, 111; first teachers, 111.
Mystery, and sex, 15.

Names, of sex organs, 148 ff.
National Education Association, resolution on sex-instruction, 232.
Nature-study, 133.
Need, of sex-instruction, 11, 19.
Neumann, H., 221.

Oliphant, James, 159.
Optimism, sex, 196.
Organization, of sex-education, 96 ff.

Parents, and daughters, 184, 190; coöperation of, 23; responsibility, 14; attitude, 30.
Parkinson, W. D., 41.
Passion, 58.
Pessimism, sex, 72, 84, 196.
Poetry, 124 ff.
Pre-adolescence, 25, 133 ff.
Problems of sex, 28 ff., 92, 95.
Promiscuity, 38.
Propagandism, needed, 28 ff.
Prophylactics, venereal, 219.
Prostitution, 48 ff., 164; protective knowledge for women, 199.

Reading, concerning perversion and vice, 51.
Refinement, of men, 167.
Religion, approach to sex-instruction, 209.
Repplier, Agnes, 203.
Reproduction, and sex, 5.
Responsibility, indirect of women, 195; individual, 18; of parents, 30.

Sanitation, and morals, 229; see also hygiene and ethics.
Self-abuse, 137 ff.

INDEX

Self-control, 70, 173, 176–182; of women, 190 ff.
Sensationalism, 233.
Sex-education, definition, 1; larger view of, 27; need of, 11; problems of, 28 ff.; relations, 4.
Sex-hygiene, 1–5; adequacy, 43; personal, 35 ff.; social, 3; and eugenics, 86; and ethics, 114, 212 ff.; personal, 98 ff.
Sex-instruction, in schools, 20, 23; in homes, 21; in high schools, 24; many-sided, 89.
Sex, meaning of the word, 6–10.
Social diseases, 166; essential knowledge to be taught, 107.
Social evil, 4, 48 ff.
Social hygiene, 3; and ethics, 101.

Societies, for sex problems, 231, 232.
Society for Prophylaxis, 62.
Super-morality, 64 ff.
Syphilis, see Diseases.

Taft, W. H., 224.
Task, of sex-education, 90.
Teachers, of sex facts, 108; for classes, 113; married women, 110; same sex as pupils, 109; undesirable, 115.
Teaching, morals, 216 ff.; personal, 205, 214.
Tennyson, and sex lessons, 125.

Vulgarity, 67 ff.

Women, and diseases, 45; instruction for, 184 ff.

Printed in the United States of America.

BIBLIOLIFE

Old Books Deserve a New Life
www.bibliolife.com

Did you know that you can get most of our titles in our trademark **EasyScript**™ print format? **EasyScript**™ provides readers with a larger than average typeface, for a reading experience that's easier on the eyes.

Did you know that we have an ever-growing collection of books in many languages?

Order online:
www.bibliolife.com/store

Or to exclusively browse our **EasyScript**™ collection:
www.bibliogrande.com

At BiblioLife, we aim to make knowledge more accessible by making thousands of titles available to you – quickly and affordably.

Contact us:
BiblioLife
PO Box 21206
Charleston, SC 29413

DOWNTOWN CAMPUS LRC

J.S. Reynolds Community College
3 7219 00172025 2

```
HQ 31 .B54 2013
Bigelow, Maurice A.
 1872-1955.
Sex education
```

DISCARDED